The literacy link

Other titles in the series

Grammar is fun (YPF8)
by Lydia Biriotti

Learning languages through games can both be fun and develop grammatical awareness! This book combines games with meticulous attention to grammar and syntax in language teaching for young children. Examples and activities are provided in French, but the ideas and methodology are applicable to other languages.

Making the link (YPF7)
by Daniel Tierney and Malcolm Hope

This book gives guidance on how to teach a foreign language to young learners by linking it to other areas of the curriculum. This approach has the advantage that the teacher may be able to reinforce in the foreign language, concepts already developed through other related curriculum work.

Let's join in! (YPF6)
by Cynthia Martin with Catherine Cheater

This book brings together a collection of rhymes, poems and songs which have proved motivating for learners from three to thirteen. It is intended as a practical resource for both specialist and non-specialist teachers of French and German at primary level and for teachers at Key Stage 3 who would like ideas to complement their coursebook. It also provides teachers of less frequently taught languages with ideas which they can adapt to their own needs.

First steps to reading and writing (YPF5)
by Christina Skarbek

This book investigates how much can be done at the early stages of foreign language teaching to prepare young learners for reading and writing. The aim is to ensure that young learners remain interested and motivated, to get them accustomed to working with written text and for them to enjoy experimenting with words.

Keep talking: teaching in the target language (YPF4)
by Peter Satchwell

This book builds on the initial experience of the primary teacher of introducing the foreign language into the classroom. It provides detailed guidance on how to ensure progression by developing the use of the language further, by encouraging pupil to teacher and pupil to pupil talk with a limited but well-planned range of the target language (examples from French and German).

Are you sitting comfortably? Telling stories to young language learners (YPF3)
by Daniel Tierney and Patricia Dobson

How to keep learners spellbound and develop their listening skills in the target language at the same time. The authors provide guidelines on the type of stories that work well in the foreign language. They look at different ways of presenting stories, preparation for storytelling and follow-up activities.

Games and fun activities (YPF2)
by Cynthia Martin

Contains many strategies and enjoyable activities which enable young learners to develop their language skills. Guidance is given on choice, preparation, organisation and management of games. Support for non-foreign languages specialists is provided through examples of target language instructions for each of the activities given and an appendix of useful teacher and pupil language in French and German.

Catching them young (YPF1)
by Peter Satchwell and June de Silva

This book provides guidance on how to integrate foreign language teaching into the primary curriculum. It suggests ways of setting up and implementing a foreign language course, covering teaching aims and methodologies, resources and course content. It addresses the issue of learner progression from primary to secondary school and contains numerous ideas for classroom activities.

early language learning

ELL is a DfES initiative managed by CILT, working in partnership with QCA, BECTA, the Central Bureau, the TTA, OFSTED and the Association for Language Learning.

Young Pathfinder 9

A CILT series for primary language teachers

The literacy link

Catherine Cheater and Anne Farren

Centre for Information
on Language Teaching and Research

The views expressed in this publication are the authors' and do not necessarily represent those of CILT.

Acknowledgements

The authors would like to offer their grateful thanks ...

For trying out some of the ideas in this book and appearing in the photographs, Annette Omri and Year 3 children from Reevy Hill Primary School, Bradford, West Yorkshire.

For practical help and advice with this book: Ute Hitchin, CILT.

Catherine would like to acknowledge her gratitude to the following ...

For instilling in me a love of reading, other languages and cultures from an early age: my parents, June and Charles Sigsworth.

For making the process of becoming literate such terrific FUN: Miss Barnes and Miss Gibbs and all staff of Margaret Allen School, Hereford.

For practical help and advice: Angela Cooper, Mary Rose, and teachers from South Gloucestershire schools.

For kinaesthetic and grammatical inspiration: Jacquie Pick and Jacqueline Dawson, Croydon LEA.

For the encouragement to write this book: Peter Satchwell, Primary Languages Network.

Anne would like to acknowledge her gratitude to Lucila Benitez, Language Officer, Consejería de Educación y Ciencia, Londres, who very kindly checked the Spanish text.

First published 2001 by the Centre for Information on Language Teaching and Research (CILT)
20 Bedfordbury, London WC2N 4LB
Copyright © Centre for Information on Language Teaching and Research 2001
Illustrations © John Richardson 2001
ISBN 1 902031 41 5
2005 2004 2003 2002 2001 / 10 9 8 7 6 5 4 3 2 1
A catalogue record for this book is available from the British Library

Cover design by Neil Alexander. Printed in Great Britain by Copyprint UK Ltd

CILT Publications are available from: **Central Books,** 99 Wallis Rd, London E9 5LN. Tel: 0845 458 9910. Fax: 0845 458 9912. Book trade representation (UK and Ireland): **Broadcast Book Services,** Charter House, 27a London Road, Croydon CR0 2RE. Tel: 020 8681 8949. Fax: 020 8688 0615.

Contents

KEY TO SYMBOLS

 There are many suggestions in this book for methods which teachers might use to develop dictionary skills in young learners. As these opportunities occur within all three strands – word, sentence and text level – this symbol highlights, at a glance, all such references.

 There are suggestions throughout this Young Pathfinder for occasions when ICT can be a helpful tool to support and reinforce learning. All such references are highlighted by use of this symbol.

Introduction: The world of language

The primary phase is the time when children's interest in and knowledge of language is being rapidly and securely developed. To discover the **world of language** can be to **open up the world**. The presence of a foreign language in the classroom gives the children a point of comparison with their own language at every possible stage, through word, sentence and text level work. Young children can develop a fascination for language if the methodology of the classroom is stimulating and involves the learners as fully as possible. To engage them as much as possible, teachers need to give the learners something to:

- look at
- imagine
- listen to
- respond to
- sort or set
- sequence
- solve
- compare
- match
- choose
- draw
- make
- count
- repeat
- read aloud
- read silently
- recite
- memorise
- write/copy write
- spell verbally or aurally
- taste
- smell
- hold
- touch
- pass to someone
- mime
- act out
- solve
- research/find out.

What do we need to bring into the classroom to help the learners to experience language in such a rich way?

- Classroom objects from other subject areas
- Cuddly toys
- Food
- Text flashcards
- Picture flashcards
- Photographs or postcards
- Alphabet letters
- Grapheme cards and letter fans
- Overhead transparencies
- Song cassettes and CDs
- Videos and DVDs
- Poems
- Stories
- CD-ROMs
- Comic books, magazines
- Worksheets
- Dictionaries and encyclopaedias.

The suggestions in this book are divided into word, sentence and text level sections, which we hope will facilitate the way of working for the class teacher, who will already be planning daily literacy work for children within these three levels. In this way, teachers will be able to make connections between literacy development in English and comparative or reinforcement work carried out in a foreign language. Teachers already familiar with the National Literacy Strategy (NLS) will understand the 'searchlight approach' which aims to balance a range of strategies which help children to deal with text:

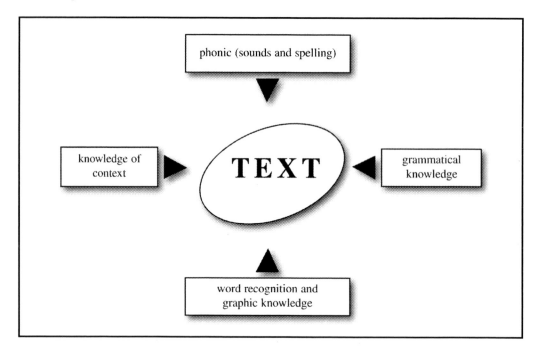

The NLS Framework itself organises teaching objectives at three different levels: word, sentence and text. '*This underlines the importance of teaching pupils to use the full range of searchlights – to tackle texts from individual words upwards and from the text downwards. While all the searchlights are important, the balance between them should vary at different stages of learning to read*' (*National Literacy Strategy*, p5).

This Young Pathfinder aims to show the teacher the beginnings of methodology which can integrate a modern foreign language into the language and literacy development of the young child. Readers may also wish to see examples of lively, interactive teaching of MFL to young learners in the video *Making it happen*, available from CILT. We hope that from these small beginnings teachers will find new pathways and strategies which can excite young learners, and support and enrich the whole experience of language and literacy development.

CILT

1. Word level

FAMILIAR AND UNFAMILIAR SOUNDS

Word level work focuses mainly on phonics, spelling and vocabulary. Through it we aim to increase children's knowledge of vocabulary, and to familiarise them with common spelling patterns, with the sounds which make up the words, and with the way in which those sounds can be represented on paper. Many children already have a well-developed awareness of the sounds which make up the English language by the time they start school, and some pupils even learn to read comparatively easily and quickly because they appear to be able to match the aural to the visual, and to match familiar words on the page with words which they know by sound.

However, not all children are sufficiently aware of the different sounds that exist in English, even when English is their home language, to be able to relate sound to symbol when they are learning to read. It can help learners considerably if sound patterns that they hear are broken down or built up, and explained in a meaningful way. Some children benefit from being shown at close range how to shape their mouth and tongue. If they have never been able to verbalise certain sounds by the time they start school, the teaching of reading is more difficult.

Misunderstandings can sometimes occur when we are not quite certain about new sounds or words, and we substitute by drawing on what we know. A little anecdote that might serve to illustrate this point is the case of the child who told her mother that she knew what God's name was. 'God's name is Peter', she said. 'How do you know this?' enquired her mother. 'Because when we are in church on Sundays, the vicar quite often says 'Thanks, Peter God''. This child was destined to keep hearing this, rather than 'Thanks be to God', unless the sounds were broken down and explained sufficiently. This example also shows how important it is to have an **accurate understanding of sounds**, which can be very closely related, in order for the **meaning** to be understood.

By means of the NLS and other opportunities, children can develop phonological awareness and spelling strategies in English. Young children are often fascinated by sounds, and we can use their enthusiasm for listening to them as a means of helping them to link sound to symbol and symbol to sound.

WHY INCLUDE A MODERN FOREIGN LANGUAGE?

Children are so interested in language when they are very young that including nursery rhymes, songs and stories, words and phrases in a foreign language in classroom activities usually presents no problems whatsoever, but rather adds to the excitement and interest. Many word, sentence and text level objectives found in the Literacy Strategy can be supported through the teaching of a modern foreign language. It can be used as a tool to help children to develop an **awareness of sounds and words**, as well as **sentence structure and grammar**. It can add another dimension to **phonic work**, as we can play with sounds for the pleasure of it without having always to be concerned with words and their meanings. **Spelling strategies**, as well as **reading strategies**, can be developed by linking the sounds of speech to the letters, which represent them in writing, i.e. phoneme/grapheme correspondences. Therefore, a foreign language can enhance the development of literacy skills by:

- adding interest and increasing motivation for language learning;
- helping children to concentrate;
- raising awareness of language in the wider world;
- developing the desire to use language as a means of communication;
- developing listening, speaking, reading and writing skills;
- developing spelling strategies;
- reinforcing similarities with mother tongue;
- highlighting differences with mother tongue;
- developing an awareness of grammar and pattern in language.

It is sometimes possible to use the foreign language to help meet Literacy Strategy objectives at the same time as they are being met in English. However, it is important to realise that the foreign language can also be used to revise and reinforce prior learning, to provide opportunities to **revisit earlier learning within a new context**, when children might resent doing so in English. In other words, the foreign language can provide the context for a 'fresh start', and **help to rescue children who might otherwise have been left behind.**

RECOGNISING AND MAKING SOUNDS

If children are to become literate, it is important that they be taught to discriminate between the separate sounds in words. Learners need to be given opportunities to listen to a variety of sounds in the language(s) with which they are working, and also to enunciate these sounds themselves so that they can feel physically what it is like to make them. These opportunities can provide a lot of fun and at the same time develop the skills of listening and speaking.

In order to support and reinforce learning in the mother tongue, it is best to look for phonemes (sounds) and graphemes (symbols) which are the same in both languages. In German there are probably more similarities with English than there are differences, so it is easy to find ways of using German to support literacy development in English. There are also many similarities in French, but examples need to be chosen carefully. For instance, the letter *s* can be used to make the sound [s], but there are many occasions when it does not make this sound.(just as there are in English). When *s* is used to make the plural of a noun in English, the sound [s] is enunciated, but when this letter performs the same function in French, the letter is not pronounced.

PEBBLE GAME

In order to help learners to identify sounds and sound patterns, they should be encouraged to make these sounds themselves. Getting children to respond to sounds they hear will help you to ensure that they have heard and recognised them.

When developing awareness of the initial sound of letters in English, and getting children to think of the sound with which a word begins, the *Pebble game* can be useful. An object is passed around the circle, indicating when it is the turn of each child to speak. It is passed around to a steady beat, in order to maintain momentum and hold the interest of the participants. The children are encouraged to think of any word they know which begins with, ends with, or contains a particular **sound**. Knowledge of words in a foreign language offers the children more scope. For instance, if we are trying to think of words which begin with the sound [m], we might think of …

match – mask – mother – Mummy – man – mop – middle – monster – make – muddle

and we could add words from our knowledge of French …
mère – Maman – monster – méchant – mange –

or our knowledge of German …
Messer – Monster – Mutter – Mutti – mache –

Children can also use examples from nursery rhymes, short poems and songs, both in English and the foreign language. Ask them to recite particular rhymes, in chorus, and to stand up or make some kind of signal when they find a word beginning with the chosen sound, e.g. [m]:

Humpty Dumpty sat on a wall.
Humpty Dumpty had a great fall.
All the king's horses and all the king's **men**…..
Couldn't put Humpty together again.

Now let's try the same thing in French, listening for a word beginning with [b]:

Deux petits escargots
Dans le jardin
*'**Bonjour**!' '**Bonjour**!'*

And in German, we'll jump up when we hear words beginning with the [k] sound:

Ein großer Hund
*Eine **kleine Katze***
*Dann **kommt** die Maus*
Und das Spiel ist aus!

Of course the same well-known rhymes can be used again and again, in order to listen for and respond to different sounds. These can be vowel sounds or consonants, and they can be sounds found within words as well as sounds which begin words.

Not only can foreign languages be used to reinforce similarities with English, but they can be used to give practice in listening for **sounds which do not exist in English**. This adds a rich new dimension to speaking and listening work. Because the learners are listening for particular sounds within a body of words they do not generally know the meaning of, the listening task can be even more focused and precise than in English.

In French, for example, there exist nasal sounds which do not exist in English:

[ɔ̃]   as in *bon, melon, concombre*

[ã]   as in *dans, sans, danse, méchant, vent, centre*

[ɛ̃]   as in *matin, lutin, main, demain, plein*

[œ̃]   as in *un, lundi, brun*

Sounds such as these, which are so different, provide an interesting focus for comparison, both in terms of the sound and of the phoneme/grapheme correspondences. If children can learn some of the rules of pronunciation of a foreign language, they will enjoy the challenge of comparing some of the French words above with the following similar English words:

melon, cucumber, dance, chant, vent, centre, main, domain, vein, sun, sum.

PHONEME/GRAPHEME GAME

This is an activity which can give children the opportunity to hear sounds, to reproduce them verbally, and to link them with a written symbol. It unites the skills of listening, speaking and responding to written symbols, and can also allow children to 'write' their own sound/speech patterns.

If you wish to practise identifying phonemes (sounds), without having to identify graphemes (symbols), then invent funny visual symbols for the sounds you choose, such as those shown below:

Encourage the children to respond to each symbol with whatever sound you want to link to it. You can play a variety of responding games, and if you wish you can develop a sense of beat, rhythm, dynamics and expression, which will add interest. You could ask the children to respond to a symbol by making the chosen sound, or you could ask the children to hold up a picture of the symbol that matches the sound. For instance, read out the following words to the children, and ask them to hold up a triangle whenever they think the word contains the phoneme [e]:

bébé – lion – manger – tortue – danser – pénible – éléphant – crocodile – mémé

Alternatively, you can match a phoneme with a physical action, to add a bit of variety. There are many physical actions that children love to perform, and listening skills can be equally well developed by asking children to respond to a sound, as they can if the children respond to a word or a phrase. Here are some suggestions using sounds found in German:

CILT

schhh ▷ action might be to mimic the action of a piston, moving both arms forwards or backwards.

tsss ▷ action might be to gently place both hands on top of head.

ei ▷ action might be to stretch upwards, placing both hands in the air.

When your purpose is to link certain phonemes to graphemes, decide on two or three sounds which you would like the children to be able to enunciate. Show the children how the sound can be written down. Here is an example using the same German sounds already mentioned:

sch ▷ is a possible grapheme in German for the sound [ʃ], as in ship or dish.

z ▷ is a possible grapheme in German for the sound [ts], as in cats or sits.

ei ▷ is a possible grapheme for the sound [aɪ], as in mine or drive.

Now write out a 'sound sequence' like the one below which you can perform by reading it. Then encourage the children to perform it with you. You can devise a symbol (such as the heart below) which indicates a pause. When they are confident, ask a child (or ask the children in groups) to devise a different sound sequence using the same graphemes.

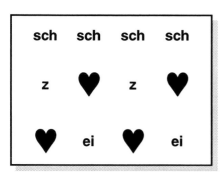

I can read letters that represent sounds

The children can also listen to sound sequences that you devise, and try to write the sequence down. In order to do this, they must know in which language they are working, and what the agreed graphemes or symbols are.

I can write a letter or grapheme in response to a sound

PHONEME OR SOUNDS GAME

To encourage children to recognise an individual phoneme or sound, we can play a listening and responding game. The children can be introduced to a range of sounds, but they have to remember which is the chosen one for that game. If we decide that the sound we are listening for today is [en], we can firstly practise chanting it aloud, rhythmically, possibly clapping as well. The teacher should try to check that all the children can enunciate the sound correctly, in order to determine that they can actually hear it correctly. Individual children should be asked to say the chosen sound.

With the class sitting in a circle, an item is passed around the circle from person to person, and each person says the chosen phoneme, [en]. When this activity has been well established, and the children are enunciating the sound correctly and confidently, allow the class to choose a consonant which can be placed in front of the sound, e.g. [b]. The circle activity is repeated but the utterance is now [ben]. Encourage the children to be alert to the initial sound changing, as whenever the teacher holds up a different 'consonant card', the utterance changes:

consonant card	utterance
l	[len]
d	[den]
z	[zen]
k	[ken]

The children can also be given opportunities to invent their own funny words, by adding any initial sound of their choosing to the selected phoneme.

Alternatively, it can be only the teacher who speaks, and the children must respond in silence. The teacher reads aloud, slowly, a medley of different sounds. Here are some examples in French:

[ɛ̃]	as in *fin*
[in]	as in *fine*
[ɑn]	as in *âne*
[wɛ̃]	as in *coin*
[ɑm]	as in *âme*
[at]	as in *pirate*
[ɔ̃]	as in *ton*
[œ̃]	as in *un*
[yn]	as in *une*

and of course [ɛn] as in *reine*, which is the sound we have chosen for today's listening activity.

Give the children two different actions to perform, for example hands on hips and hands on heads. To keep to only two actions keeps the activity simple and manageable, and gives a very visible support to all the children involved. Tell the children to put their hands on their hips when they hear any sound which is not [ɛn], and to put their hands on their heads when they hear [ɛn].

CILT

Children who are initially slow to discriminate between the different sounds should feel supported by the majority who will hopefully be performing the actions correctly, and they should gradually be able to follow what is going on. In fact the visible actions should help all the children to discriminate between the sounds, as they notice which action is associated with which sound.

You must judge the pace of such work, taking into account the age and experience of the children, but when the children appear to be coping confidently with the activity in this form, it can speeded up and can then be played while the children have their eyes closed. If the children can perform the actions correctly with eyes closed, then they are showing that they are responding only to the stimulus of the sound and no longer relying on visual support.

If some children in the class are very good at this kind of activity, they can be chosen to demonstrate to the rest of the class at high speed, in a kind of knock-out in the style of *Simon says*.

The sound which the teacher wishes to focus on can be changed whenever necessary, and well-known sounds can be revisited from time to time.

IDENTIFYING SOUNDS IN A POEM

Here is a French poem in which the sound [ɛn] occurs frequently:

Marylène la baleine
A beaucoup de peine
La murène sa marraine
A croqué à perdre haleine
Ses deux mitaines de laine
'J'avais faim!' dit l'énergumène
Sans gêne …

From *Phonétines* © Castor Poche, Flammarion, 1992

It can prompt the children to use and extend the skills they developed in the phoneme/sounds game.

If you can read the poem aloud confidently, at a slow pace, the same phoneme game can be played. If you prefer, the poem can be recorded by a foreign language assistant at an agreed pace. This time, instead of responding to the sound [ɛn] amongst a medley of unrelated phonemes, the children are doing so whilst listening to an extended piece of spoken language in which the sound [ɛn] forms part of several different words.

The children can learn to recognise which words contain the sound [ɛn], and which do not. Playing the same game, you can select any words at random from the poem to read aloud. If the word contains the chosen sound, the children can put their hands on their head; if not, then hands on hips.

The *True/false echoing game* is variation on this activity. Ask the pupils to echo back to you, in chorus, whichever words from the poem you choose to say at random. Then stipulate that they must only echo the words containing the chosen phoneme, and remain silent (performing a silly action?) when you say a word that does not contain the chosen phoneme.

Other activities that encourage children to listen for and respond to particular sounds:

- Pass an object round the circle as the poem is being read. The object can only be passed on when the chosen sound is heard. At the end of the poem, count how many people have held the object.

- Each time the sound is heard, the next person in the circle stands up. Count how many people are standing at the end of the poem.

- Choose a child (or small group) who will take one pace forward every time the sound is heard. Ask the children to guess whether or not the child will reach the window/ reach the door/ have to leave the classroom/etc by the end of the poem.

- Working in small groups, the children use lego or multilink, linking another piece each time they hear the chosen phoneme. Read the poem several times for them to check. At the end of the poem, count how many pieces of multilink have been assembled by each group.

Over a period of time, the children will be able to learn the poem by heart and to recite it from memory. They should be given frequent opportunities to recite the poem in chorus and then learn to respond to the words of the poem syllable by syllable in various ways:

- As they recite the poem, they clap their hands on each syllable which is not [ɛn], and put their hands on their head for [ɛn].

- Sitting in a circle, all children recite the poem at a moderate to slow pace. This activity is rather like *Pass-the-parcel,* but the children are actually passing a cuddly toy or soft ball around the circle. Every time a syllable is enunciated, the ball is passed one place along the circle to the next person. But every time the chosen phoneme is enunciated, the ball must change direction and be passed back the other way.

I can recite English rhymes and poems from memory

I can recite Spanish rhymes and poems from memory

CiLT

DISCRIMINATING SOUNDS

In order to encourage children to discriminate between different sounds in words, we can develop further the activities mentioned earlier in this section. Once again, they can perform simple physical actions to indicate when they can hear a particular sound. These sounds can be formed of single letters or of a combination of letters, and the actions can be as simple as putting up your hand.

The teacher might say 'Put up your hand when you hear a word containing the sound [p]'. The teacher can then read aloud a series of words, such as ….

lapin,	*chien,*	*peinture,*
écureuil,	*perroquet,*	*kangourou,*
loup,	*serpent,*	*zèbre …*

or in German …

Panther,	*Kaninchen,*	*Hund,*
Spinne,	*Spaß,*	*Käse,*
Pause,	*Pumpernickel,*	*Mappe …*

and in Spanish …

pierna,	*boca,*	*mano,*
manzana,	*fresa,*	*pera,*
gato,	*pez,*	*pájaro …*

By asking the children to put up their hand, the teacher can see quickly and easily if the children are able to hear individual sounds in words.

I can hear the phonemes in words

Comparisons between English and the foreign language should be made as often as possible. Explore with the children whether a particular sound, which they have identified either in English or in the foreign language, actually exists in the other language. There are many sounds that exist across a range of languages, and some sounds which do not pass from one language to another.

For example, the following sound exists in French but not in English:
[y] as in **tu**, s**u**per, **u**ne, l**u**ne.

This sound exists in English, but not in German:
[θ] as in **th**ink, **th**anks, **th**istle.

This next sound appears in Spanish but not English:
the phoneme [ɲ], graphically represented as ñ as in espa**ñ**ol, Espa**ñ**a.

PASSIVE LISTENING

Many opportunities for passive listening arise during the course of the school day. There may be times when the children are engaged in practical activities such as painting or constructing, when it would be appropriate to play some background music quietly. There is also sometimes an opportunity at the start of the school day, if children are allowed into the classroom before registration, and can engage in quiet play or activity of some kind under supervision. If this 'background music' were sometimes to be songs in the foreign language, it would allow the children to become familiar with the style, rhythm, beat and possibly words of the foreign language songs.

  ## ALPHABETIC KNOWLEDGE

Alphabetic knowledge is one of the learning objectives of the Literacy Strategy. This knowledge is vital if pupils are to learn how to use dictionaries, either mono-lingual or bi-lingual, and encyclopaedias. If children are to become successful independent learners, they need to be able to access information contained in all kinds of books, and alphabetic and numeric knowledge is vital when understanding how to use a contents section, glossary and index.

Activities that reinforce alphabetic knowledge should be used frequently in the mother tongue, and as the children become familiar with the foreign language these activities can be expanded. Regular saying and/or singing of the alphabet in English, as well as in the foreign language, is important for the on-going development of dictionary skills.

Older children who appear to be confident in their knowledge of the English alphabet will enjoy learning a foreign language alphabet, and making comparisons with English. It is not recommended that the foreign language alphabet be taught to children who are not yet secure in their alphabetic knowledge of English, as this might cause confusion. However, if a foreign alphabet is learned at a later stage it can be used to reinforce and develop alphabet and dictionary skills that children might feel they have covered (but not necessarily mastered) in mother-tongue.

There are many commercially available cassettes and videos, which teach the correct pronunciation of the alphabet through songs (see Appendix 1 on p76). Here is a pronunciation guide:

French			Ⓐ ah	Ⓑ beh
Ⓒ ceh	Ⓓ deh	Ⓔ euh	Ⓕ ef	Ⓖ shay
Ⓗ ash	Ⓘ ee	Ⓙ shee	Ⓚ ka	Ⓛ el
Ⓜ em	Ⓝ en	Ⓞ oh	Ⓟ peh	Ⓠ koo
Ⓡ er	Ⓢ ess	Ⓣ teh	Ⓤ oo	Ⓥ veh
Ⓦ doobl-veh	Ⓧ eeks	Ⓨ eegrek	Ⓩ zed	

German			Ⓐ ah	Ⓑ beh
Ⓒ tseh	Ⓓ deh	Ⓔ eh	Ⓕ ef	Ⓖ geh
Ⓗ ha	Ⓘ ee	Ⓙ yot	Ⓚ ka	Ⓛ el
Ⓜ em	Ⓝ en	Ⓞ oh	Ⓟ peh	Ⓠ koo
Ⓡ er	Ⓢ es	Ⓣ teh	Ⓤ oo	Ⓥ fow
Ⓦ weh	Ⓧ ix	Ⓨ üpsilon	Ⓩ tset	

Spanish			Ⓐ ah	Ⓑ beh
Ⓒ theh	Ⓓ deh	Ⓔ eh	Ⓕ efeh	Ⓖ geh
Ⓗ acheh	Ⓘ ee	Ⓙ hota	Ⓚ kah	Ⓛ eleh
Ⓜ emeh	Ⓝ eneh	Ⓞ oh	Ⓟ peh	Ⓠ cooh
Ⓡ erreh	Ⓢ eseh	Ⓣ the	Ⓤ oo	Ⓥ ooveh
Ⓦ ooveh dobleh	Ⓧ ekis	Ⓨ ee greeaygah	Ⓩ thetah	

As well as learning to recognise the letters by their sound, and learning to pronounce them in the foreign language, children can be helped by playing with the shape of each letter. In the *Air writing game*, invite a child to stand in front of the class facing the board and to write 'in the air' any letter of the alphabet. This is easier if the child is facing away from the class, so that he can write the letter in the normal way.

Writing on backs is a similar activity. Choose three children to come to the front of the class to start the game off. The 'guesser' stands facing away from the class. The 'card holder' selects an alphabet letter from the pile of alphabet cards, and in silence shows it only to the 'scribe' and to the rest of the class. The scribe then 'writes' the chosen letter, using a finger, on the back of the 'guesser'. When the letter has been guessed correctly, move the children along quickly. The scribe becomes the guesser, the card-holder becomes the scribe, and the previous guesser chooses (from the class) a new card-holder who comes to the front of the class. The whole process is repeated.

Great fun can also be had with a game of *Letter shapes*. Allow the children to work alone, in pairs or in small groups, to use their bodies to create a letter of the alphabet. After a short preparation time, these can then be shown to the rest of the class, who can guess the letter.

Very young learners enjoy playing *Letters in the bag*. A bag containing letters of the alphabet (on small cards, or fridge magnet letters, or *Scrabble* letters) is passed around the circle while the music plays. Whenever the music stops, the child holding the bag pulls out a letter and names it aloud. If correct, the child keeps the letter, if incorrect, the letter is put back in the bag. The music plays again and the game continues until the bag is empty. If the teacher wishes, the music can be songs which the children know and can sing along with. The teacher need only place inside the bag letters which the children have learned.

It is possible to begin using the foreign language alphabet to develop spelling skills even before the children have been taught the entire foreign language alphabet. Children can enjoy learning to spell a small bank of familiar words, and they usually find this very empowering. This skill can initially be taught and practised passively, with the teacher spelling aloud words, which the children know well. A good place to start is with the names of children in the class. The teacher can call out in French ' *J majuscule – o – h – n* ' and the children should be able to work out that the name is 'John'. Children can show their understanding by pointing to the person whose name has been spelt; in this way, all the children are involved in the activity, and those whose spelling skills are slower to develop can be encouraged and supported by joining in with the pointing! You can gradually ask the children if any of them would like to try repeating the spelling.

Naming each letter of the alphabet in both upper and lower case is a useful skill, which can be used by children when they spell words aloud. Identifying upper and lower case letters correctly will reinforce the idea that proper nouns must begin with a capital letter. In fact, those children who learn German as a foreign language begin to understand very quickly which words are nouns because they all begin with a capital letter.

It is not difficult to identify upper and lower case letters in the foreign language:

English	▷	capital A	small a
French	▷	*A majuscule*	*a minuscule*
German	▷	*A groß*	*a klein*
Spanish	▷	*A mayuscula*	*a minúscula*

Older pupils might not consider this a worthwhile activity in mother tongue, as they know that they have progressed beyond this level in English, but in a foreign language it is amazing how enthusiastically they want to participate. This is another example of how a foreign language can be used as a tool to reinforce prior learning and skills.

Once the children can cope with this activity in a passive way, they will gradually be able to spell aloud some of the known words for their friends to guess. Writing practice can also be given by dictating known words or phrases to the children, or by groups dictating words to others in the form of a competition.

I can write a letter when I hear its sound

CiLT

It is motivating and encouraging for children to be able to read on sight a range of words with which they are familiar, for example the words for greetings or the names of colours. When the children are involved in text level work, for instance from a big book or from an overhead transparency, they can easily identify certain well-known words:

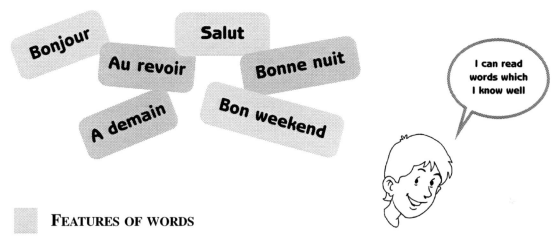

Bonjour

Salut

Au revoir

Bonne nuit

A demain

Bon weekend

I can read words which I know well

FEATURES OF WORDS

By means of a foreign language, children can also be made aware of the critical features of words, such as the number of syllables a words has, the length of the word and the combination of vowels and consonants. Once the children are familiar with the concept of vowels and consonants in English, they can be given opportunities to find vowels and consonants in words in the foreign language as well as in English. Such opportunities arise frequently, and in many contexts.

VOWEL/CONSONANT DISCRIMINATION GAME

The purpose of this activity is simply to provide opportunities for the children to discriminate between vowels and consonants. Give each child two cards, one displaying the word voyelle and the other consonne.

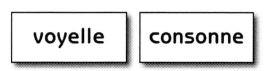

voyelle   consonne

Then say at random a range of letters, and ask the children to hold up one of their cards showing whether they think you have said a vowel or a consonant. You can also play this game to practise recognition of the letters by holding up an alphabet card so that the children do not hear, but just read the letters. A third possibility is to do both: to show and pronounce the letter.

You can also display the first names of children in the class on flashcards:

Il y a combien de voyelles dans ce mot?   Deux voyelles.
Et combien de consonnes?   Cinq consonnes.

Wieviele Vokale gibt es?   Zwei Vokale.
Und wieviele Konsonante?   Fünf Konsonante.

¿Cuántas vocales contiene esta palabra?   Dos vocales.
¿Y cuántas consonantes?   Cinco consonantes.

Richard

The children can manage this activity in the foreign language if they know numbers for counting, and the words for vowels and consonants. To develop this idea further, when the children know the alphabet in the target language, they can also name the letters …

Deux voyelles: i, a. Cinq consonnes: r, c, h, r, d.

SYLLABLES

Before the children can understand or express verbally the concept of how many syllables are in words, you could play the *Syllables clapping game*. Ask the children to suggest which word (from a certain group) you could be clapping if you give two claps. Answering in French, the children could say '*lapin, chenille, panthère, chameau,* or *cochon*'. It is also important to play the same game in English, as the children will notice differences and become more aware of the features of the words in English.

The game can develop the children's thinking as deeply as you wish in relation to the critical features of words, as you can group the features together. You could ask them to think of a noun which is masculine, has two vowels, one consonant and one accent (*âne*); or a noun which has two syllables in English, but only one in French (donkey/*âne*); or which has one syllable in English but two in French (pig/*cochon*).

When the children are used to playing with words in this way, you can make the game harder. The following activity is a useful 'settler' when you want to encourage the children to think quietly about language. This activity explores the features of certain words in both English and the foreign language. It is called *What do these words have in common?* and can be played with any set of words you choose. The children sit in a circle, with the chosen words available in the middle of the circle. The teacher selects picture cards and displays them in the middle of the circle.

CILT

What does this word have in common in French and in English? Possible answers could be: it has three syllables in both languages, it has eight letters, it begins with a vowel, it ends with a consonant, it has three vowels, it has five consonants.

When the children are used to seeing (and reading) the words for the animals, you can take this activity further, for example:

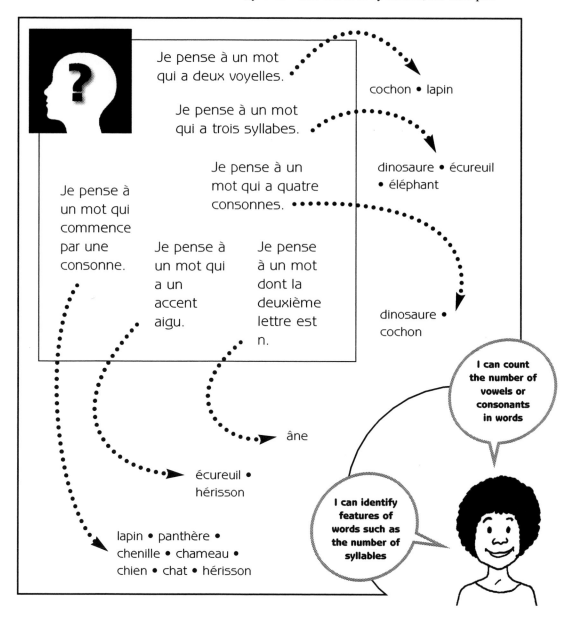

In this way, you are encouraging the children to investigate the features of words. It is important to make children aware of these features, as this can help them to develop successful spelling strategies as well as dictionary skills.

DICTIONARY SKILLS

Helping the children to become confident manipulators of words in more than one language will show them that their own language is only one communication system amongst many, and that they can access information using identical processes in more than one language. It is important that children are taught dictionary skills, and it must be recognised that dictionary skills are a vital tool not only in a mono-lingual environment, but also in a multi-lingual context. Dictionary skills can become more advanced as the learner's literacy skills become more developed.

Frequent practice can be given in putting words into dictionary order, even before the children are accustomed to using real dictionaries.

There is usually an alphabet frieze displayed on the wall of KS1 classrooms, as a reference point for the children. At a glance, they can see the correct sequence of letters in the alphabet. When working on letter sounds at the beginning of words, for instance [k] as in 'cow' and [d] as in 'dog', listening activities can give the children practice in identifying those sounds. When they then learn to identify which letter of the alphabet is associated with the initial sound in these words, they can check against the alphabet frieze to learn in which order they would appear in the alphabet (and hence in a dictionary).

You may have a collection of items such as a duck, dolphin, dinosaur, donkey, dog, crocodile, crab, cow, cat and clown. These can be in the form of realia (cuddly toys are usually popular!), or pictorial flashcards. In English, these words begin with only one of two sounds, [k] and [d]. In order to use a foreign language to practise this kind of listening skill, you would need to gather a similar set if items or pictures in your target language. The children must be very familiar with their names in the foreign language before dictionary skills can be practised.

ACTIVITIES TO PLAY WITH THE INITIAL SOUNDS IN WORDS

- Hold up any of the ten toys at random, and ask the children to enunciate the initial sound in chorus, or individually.

- Alternatively, ask the children to show whether they think the word begins with **c** or **d** by holding up their letter fans.

- When the pupils are more confident and can respond individually, play a musical game. The children sit in a circle, holding all the toys. While the music is playing, they pass the toys around the circle in the same direction. When the music stops, the teacher names any one of the toys. All children holding a toy which begins with the same letter must place it in the middle of the circle before the teacher can count to three. The toys are gathered up, and the game recommences. As the learners' knowledge of vocabulary increases, this game can be played with cuddly toys beginning with a variety of initial sounds.

- Sorting activity: The children can be asked to sort the items by their initial sound. This can still be done as a whole class activity if the teacher selects one child each time, or asks a small group to demonstrate in front of the others. The items can be sorted on to two mats, one labelled c and the other d.

These activities are ideal to play in KS1 at the time when children are learning to discriminate between different sounds in English. They will, however, also be enjoyed by much older children, say in Years 2 to 4, where they would serve to reinforce prior learning through a different medium.

Dictionary skills can be practised form an early stage in the learners' foreign language development, if the children are asked to select particular toys and to place them into dictionary order. For instance, ask the children '*Je voudrais un lapin et un âne*'. Then ask if anyone can place the toys correctly into dictionary order.

We have seen how younger children can sequence and sort by the initial letter of the word, even using realia rather than looking at the text words. Older children also need regular practice in sorting and sequencing words. For instance, they can sort the following text words, on flashcards, into alphabetical order …

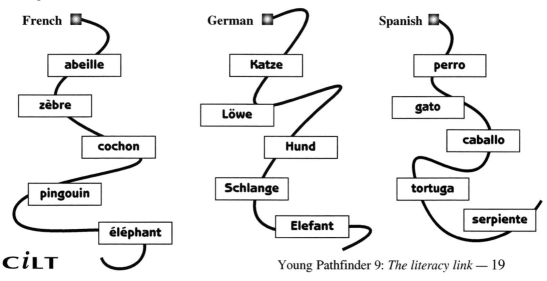

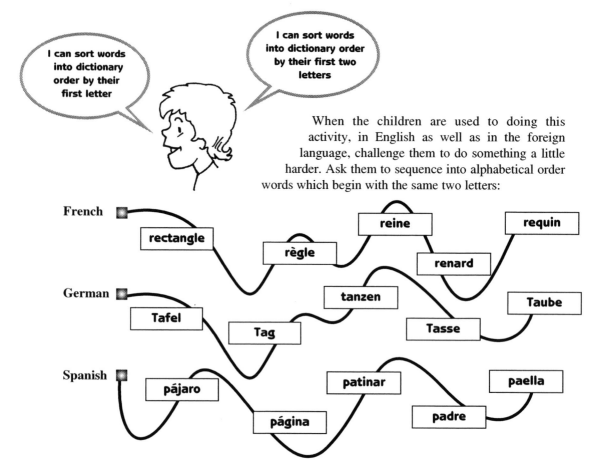

When the children are used to doing this activity, in English as well as in the foreign language, challenge them to do something a little harder. Ask them to sequence into alphabetical order words which begin with the same two letters:

When the children have understood the need to sequence words not only by their first letter, but also by their second, the process can become increasingly more complex, e.g. sorting words which begin with the same three or more letters:

Such dictionary activities are now frequently done in Literacy Hour, in English, with children in Years 3 and 4. Children who are given the opportunity to practise this skill in a foreign language might realise how valuable the skill itself is; that a system which operates in English can also operate in other languages, and that working in another language is accessible to them.

These dictionary activities, which make use of flashcards bearing words chosen by the teacher, can easily be built into a KS 2 scheme of work. By the time children are in Year 6, they should be able to sort any words into dictionary order, and should be able to use real dictionaries for a variety of purposes. Therefore, Year 3 children could be given regular practice in sorting words beginning with the same first letter, Year 4 children could sort words beginning with the same first two letters, and Year 6 children could sort words beginning with the same three or more letters. Additionally, older children could be given opportunities to practise using a dictionary by being asked to make lists of words which begin with the same two, three or four letters.

Frequent practice of this kind will allow children to:

- find words in mono-lingual or bi-lingual dictionaries;
- find meanings in mono-lingual or bi-lingual dictionaries;
- access information in encyclopaedias and other non-fiction sources;
- locate books by author in a library.

MAKING A DICTIONARY

The sorting and sequencing activities referred to are a very practical way of showing children the explicit steps needed in order to find words in a dictionary. It can also be helpful to give children the opportunity to make their own dictionaries to which they can refer whenever they wish.

In KS1 and with learners in Years 3 and 4 who are only just beginning to use text as part of their work in a foreign language, a whole-class dictionary can be made and added to whenever the opportunity arises. If stored in a large ring-binder, it will be easy to insert and remove pages when opportunities arise. This kind of dictionary is 'personalised' by the class in that it grows as the children's vocabulary grows, and it also provides a central point of reference for all children in the class, giving them practice in using non-fiction material to check words and spellings.

When the children know the cuddly toys well, by naming them correctly and confidently, they might like to make their own dictionary, which classifies their own bank of words. There are various practical ways of putting the dictionary together. Children's paintings or drawings can be used directly, or can be scanned in to the computer to be used as copies, or pictures can be cut from magazines.

If you wish to use ICT in order to teach the children how to work with text and pictures together, you could either photograph all of the cuddly toys with a digital camera and store them on the hard drive, or photograph them with an ordinary camera and scan the pictures in. Alternatively you might be able to find versions of all the toys on clipart, or you might scan in paintings of the toys that have been produced by the children. When you have decided on your picture format, you can decide at what level you think it is appropriate for the children to identify the words. The examples below assume that the children are working in French.

Word identification can be by the first letter only,

or can show the whole word,

or give whichever details about the word which you want the children to be aware of, such as the type of word (noun, verb, adjective, etc) and the gender if appropriate:

The class dictionaries can become more complex over a period of time. If the children are using the ICT methods above, they can easily make an English version of the same dictionary, in other words two separate mono-lingual dictionaries at this stage rather than one bi-lingual dictionary.

You could have a little warm-up activity every day, choosing certain cuddly toys to be placed into dictionary order. The sequence will be different depending on whether you play the game in English or in a foreign language.

This activity can be illustrated for the children as often as needed, simply by selecting one or two toys or children.

Here are two toys, a tortoise and a frog. Place them in front of the children in the reading direction, and ask the children to think about which order they should be in according to the alphabet. Ask a child to put them into the correct order. Then repeat the activity in the foreign language. In French, in this case, *grenouille* and *tortue* would be in the same order as frog and tortoise. If you also do this activity with two children rather than two cuddly toys, putting them into dictionary order by their first name, you can really engage the children in the activity and help them to remember alphabetical order in a personal way.

You can then illustrate the next step by selecting two children or toys whose names begin with the same initial letter. Left we have fish and frog.

Why is it more difficult to know in which order to place them? Because we have to look beyond the first letter of the word. The children will work this out by checking with the alphabet frieze. If we then repeat the activity in French, we discover that they do not have the same initial letters as in English, as they become *poisson* and *grenouille*. Therefore, we must reverse the sequence.

If we then choose kangaroo and camel …

… we remember that the sound [k] can be made in more than one way in English, and that these words each begin with different letters even though they begin with the same sound. In English, we would sequence them as camel and kangaroo, in French we have *chameau* and *kangourou*, in German *Kamel* and *Känguruh*, and in Spanish *camello* and *canguro*.

CiLT

DICTIONARY PROJECTS

These can be based on any topic or theme. You might possibly even use the children themselves, placing them into dictionary order by their first name. You can make a class dictionary using ICT, by putting digital photographs of each child into dictionary order by first letter. However, this can require a complex understanding of alphabetical order, as sometimes there are several names beginning with the same first, second or even third letter (Adam, Andrea, Andrew, Ann, Anne, Anthony, …). It is a very valuable activity, which can help the children to understand how to sequence words by alphabetical order.

| **Class picture**

 Class 2C Dictionary | 
 Adam | 
 Andrea | 
 Andrew | 
 Anne | 
 Anthea |

Schools linked with partner schools abroad can exchange such class dictionaries by e-mail. Dictionary work across the curriculum can be developed from reception up to Year 6, and can become more complex and sophisticated as the learners' understanding increases. By exchanging dictionaries once a term, or twice a year, with a partner class abroad, your children have an opportunity to create a dictionary on a topic directly related to their learning, and then the opportunity to use a dictionary created by their peers in another country. Even if the received dictionary is in a language which the children are not learning formally, there are many useful literacy links which can be drawn from it.

 ## RHYMING PATTERNS

A song, with which the children become familiar through passive listening, can gradually be used by the teacher to develop focused listening skills, reading and writing. On the following page is an example in French, taken from the CD *Chansons no. 5* by Henri Dès (see Appendix 1 on p76). However, the principle can be applied using any song text and audio material which is available to the teacher:

Ma forêt

Refrain:

Quand je me promène au fond de la forêt
Je ne vais pas très très loin.
Et si je t'emmène au fond de la forêt
Tu verras mes jolis coins.

Il y a des oiseaux,
Des petits, des gros,
Mais y'a pas, mais y'a pas de
perroquets.
Dans d'autres pays
Y'en a des jolis
Qui se parlent sans arrêt.

Y'a des écureuils
Cachés dans les feuilles
Mais y'a pas, mais y'a pas de koalas.
Dans les pays chauds
Y'en a des très beaux
J'en ai jamais vu par là.

Il y a des serpents,
Des petits, des grands,
Mais j'ai pas, mais j'ai pas vu de boas.
Dans d'autres pays
Y'en a des jolis
Qui s'enroulent autour de toi.

Over a period of time, you can select activities with a variety of different purposes, using this song as the foreign language stimulus. These activities would help to consolidate learning in the Literacy Strategy word level objective *'Pupils should be taught to rhyme through recognising, exploring and working with rhyming patterns.'*

ACTIVITY 1: RECOGNISING WORDS HEARD IN A SONG

Picture response

The following words from the song can easily be represented on picture flashcards, and held up by the children working in pairs or groups as they are heard in the song. To start with, just choose a word from the first verse (e.g. *perroquet*), show the children a flashcard of a parrot and another of a crocodile. Ask them to listen to the verse, and tell you which of those two words they could hear.

Text response

The same activity can be done when you want the children to work with text, using words which they can read. They can use the same ones as on the picture flashcards above, and add some more:

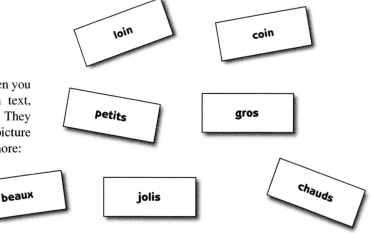

loin

coin

petits

gros

beaux

jolis

chauds

The children could work in small groups, with each group having a set of text flashcards, with some words taken from the song and others which are not found in the song. Allow the children to hear the song several times, and to work collaboratively within their groups to try and decide which words they can hear. Finally, with the whole class, compare the results of each group. Play the song again, and indicate to the children each time one of their words is sung.

ACTIVITY 2

Using both the text and the picture flashcards, the teacher and children can identify rhyming words heard in the song. The picture flashcards which identify rhyming words are …

écureuils – feuilles   koalas – boas

The text flashcards which identify rhyming words are …

loin – coins   oiseaux – gros – beaux – chauds   écureuils – feuilles
pays – jolis   koalas – boas – toi – par là   perroquets – arrêt

If the children know the song well, and can read these words, they should be able to sort the words into rhyming groups by remembering the sound of the word. The teacher and children can then use the results of the matching up in order to discover or to remember information about the written language, such as grapheme/phoneme correspondences, and similarities and differences when compared with English.

I can recognise rhyming words in poems and songs

I can read words in a poem or song

I can find groups of rhyming words in poems or songs

Allow the children to collect individual sounds, words, short phrases, sentences, rhyming words, poems and short stories which they enjoy, and provide them with opportunities to access these and re-visit them frequently.

ACTIVITY 3

Using key words from the song text, the children can find other known words that rhyme with them. For instance, if a word such as *oiseaux* is selected from the song text and read aloud, the children might be able to suggest rhymes such as: *gâteau, chapeau, moineau, bateau, cadeau, crapaud, rameau, drapeau, poireau.*

These rhymes could be selected by memory from a bank of known words, thus relying on the ear, or from text flashcards displaying words which are not necessarily known to the children, thus practising reading skills. For example, ask the children how many words they can select from the pile opposite, which they think might rhyme with *oiseaux*:

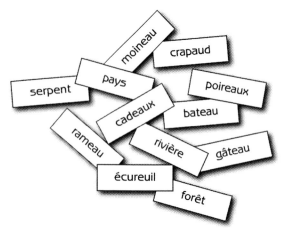

ACTIVITY 4

When children are familiar with words such as those in activity 3, they can play with the sound of the words by being challenged to find onsets to match rimes*, and rimes to match onsets. For instance, you could ask them to keep the rime in bat**eau**, and find different onsets for it:

rime	▷	onset
une	▷	*br**une**, l**une**, pr**une***
eau	▷	*b**eau**, p**eau**, s**eau**, v**eau***
ont	▷	*m**ont**, p**ont**, s**ont***
age	▷	*c**age**, g**age**, n**age**, p**age**, r**age**, s**age***

A song which could provide opportunities for the same activities in German is *Clown Sporelli* by Lore Kleikamp and Detlev Jöcker, from *Detlev Jöcker, seine schönsten Lieder* (see Appendix 1 on p76).

There are many sets of rhyming words:

Sporelli – Tarantelli	*Nas' – Glas*	*singt – bringt*
Wasserfass – nass	*Ball – Knall*	*zieht – Lied*
riesengroß – bloß	*auch – Bauch*	

---

* The NLS tells us
(NLS, p84): *the onset of a word or syllable is the initial consonant or consonant cluster: clang; trike; sun. Some words or syllables have no onset: or; use; out; aw/ful; in/side.*
(NLS, p87) *that part of a word or syllable which contains the vowel and final consonant cluster if there is one: at in cat; orn in horn; ow in cow. Some words consist of rime only: or; ate; eel.*

CiLT

For songs in Spanish, those of Rosa Leon are always a favourite. The traditional nonsense song *Debajo un botón* which she sings is one that children love to sing or chant, as the rhythms and rhymes are such fun. The activities illustrated in the examples above would equally apply here:

Debajo un botón ────

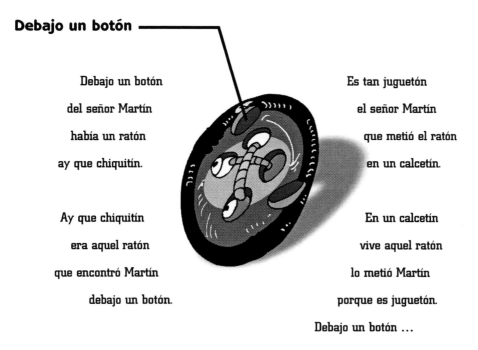

Debajo un botón

del señor Martín

había un ratón

ay que chiquitín.

Ay que chiquitín

era aquel ratón

que encontró Martín

debajo un botón.

Es tan juguetón

el señor Martín

que metió el ratón

en un calcetín.

En un calcetín

vive aquel ratón

lo metió Martín

porque es juguetón.

Debajo un botón ...

Rhythm and beat of language

Using poems which the children know well enough to recite frequently by heart, practice can be given in recognising the **rhythm** of the words, i.e. the syllables, and also the **beat.** The rhythm, as we have seen, can be established by clapping the syllables of the words as they are spoken. Knowledge of the beat of the language can be gained by clapping, tapping or conducting, in the same way that one might tap out the beat of a piece of music.

Here is an example of this using a traditional German song/poem *Es war eine Mutter*, which is in 3/4 time:

3 / 1 2 3 / 1 2 3 / 1 2 3 / 1 2 3 /
Es / war ein-e / Mut-ter, die / hat-te vier / Kin-der, den /

1 2 3 / 1 2 3 / 1 2 3 / 1 2
Früh-ling, den / Som-mer, den / Herbst und den / Winter.

The bar lines are shown between the words, and the numbers above the words indicate on which beat of the bar the word falls. Because the structure of the song is very simple, the rhythm is not complicated and matches the beat of the song.

Similarly, here is an example in French of a traditional song which is in 4/4 time:

```
1       2     3 4 /   1   2   3   4
Pomme de reinette et / pomme d'a -pi  -, /

1   2  3  4 / 1 2 3 4
Ta-pis tap-is / rou – ge – , /

1       2     3 4 /   1   2   3   4
Pomme de reinette et / pomme d'a -pi  -, /

1    2 3  4  / 1 – – –
Ta-pis ta-pis / gris.
```

In this song, the rhythm of the words is different from the beat, so the children will notice a difference between clapping out the syllables to illustrate the rhythm, and beating the time of the song. This can be reinforced both visually and aurally if the teacher divides the class into two groups, one conducting or marking the beat of the song, while the other claps the rhythm.

Children can learn to clap the **rhythm** of any poem in order to feel the rhythm of the words in the language. They can also clap the **beat** of any poem as they recite it in the same way that they might clap the beat in a piece of music. This can be done at a slow, moderate or fast tempo, and the pitch and dynamics of the voice can be varied to provide interest.

Spanish is a syllable-rhythm based language rather than one where the rhythm is based on stress, as is the case with English. The rhythm in this rhyme can be linked to bouncing a ball:

> Mi pelote salta y bota,
> Si se rompe tengo otra
> Mi pelota ya no bota
> Mi papa me compra otra.

This kind of activity, performed regularly in both the mother tongue and in the foreign language, will give children an opportunity to develop a keen ear for the sound of the language: to listen for the shape and rhythm of words, and to discriminate between the different sounds in words.

I can clap the number of syllables in words

I can group together words which have the same number of syllables

I can count the number of syllables

CiLT

2. Sentence level

Sentence level work focuses on grammar and punctuation.It is at this level that teachers can enable pupils to use some of the knowledge and skills they are developing at word level, and begin to put words into a meaningful context. It is important that children are taught how words fit together to make a sentence, and that the syntax used in English is not necessarily the same in other languages. Observation of the syntax of other languages can help children to identify the features of syntax in English, as they become aware of the similarities and differences. Understanding of pattern in language, knowledge of grammar and punctuation, can be supported by using examples taken from other languages.

We have seen in Chapter 1 how much word level work can come from within a text. Word, sentence and text levels are closely interrelated, and the teacher cannot help children to develop literacy in an overall sense unless the learning is linked through all three strands.

It is sometimes felt that, although it is easy for young children to learn how to label individual items either verbally or in writing, it is very difficult or even impossible to teach them how to construct sentences or to express ideas using larger 'chunks' of language. However, frequent opportunities to work with sentences, both in English as well as in other languages, will help to give the children the confidence that they can work in this way and be **successful**.

Text level work can certainly help the children to acquire the idea of expressing themselves using sentences. If the children learn poems, rhymes or songs by heart, they are acquiring the ability to link words together in a meaningful way. If they can be taught to recite what they have learnt using the correct intonation, rhythm and expression, then they are already developing a feeling for how the language should sound. They are learning that sentences, and phrases contained within them, have their own particular musical shape. It might be said that listening to a foreign language provides a very useful context for identifying sentences, as each sentence can be picked out simply by its musical shape, without the listener being sidetracked by the meaning of the words. Children need opportunities to hear the language modelled at text level, in order that they themselves will be able to read aloud, using expression appropriate to the grammar and punctuation of the text.

It is as important for learners to develop an awareness of how a sentence can 'sound', as it is for them to develop an awareness of the sounds within words. Provide the children with regular opportunities to hear and to recite more extended pieces of language, and to identify the sentences within them.

Initially, read out some short poems, or paragraphs from stories, and ask the children to tell you how many sentences they can hear. You can use responding activities, similar to those mentioned in Chapter 1, to encourage them to make a physical response at the start and end of each sentence. Train them to hear the shape of the sentence by exaggerating the rising and falling pitch of the voice and by pausing for longer than is usual between each sentence. Encourage the children to identify the features they can hear, and to differentiate between questions and statements in the foreign language by demonstrating the rising intonation which can be heard in questions, and the quizzical facial expression which can be seen.

When you are showing the children the text, by means of a big book or on an overhead transparency, you can repeat this activity but reinforce it visually with clues within the text which identify the sentences. This, in turn, will gradually help the children read the language aloud using meaningful expression. Teach them to notice punctuation within texts, and discuss how this helps the text to make sense. It is clearly very important that the children learn the English terminology for punctuation, but giving them the opportunity of finding punctuation in foreign language texts and using terminology in the foreign language, will provide a new context for such learning and will show the children that different languages have many common features, as well as some interesting differences.

The children can notice, for instance, features of questions in different languages:

'Where do you live?' she asked.
–*Où habites-tu? demanda-t-elle.*
«*Où habites-tu?*» *demanda-t-elle.*
«*Wo wohnst du?*» *fragte sie.*
– *¿Dónde vives? – preguntó.*

Learners might notice similarities and differences such as whether or not direct speech is indicated by speech marks, the style of the speech marks, the word order of the verb and the pronoun both within and following the direct speech, and the style and position of the question mark.

It is important to allow the children frequent opportunities to read aloud, both in chorus and individually, so that they can learn to put appropriate expression into their speaking. Let them hear the language modelled, either by you or a foreign language assistant or on an audio tape, and to mimic the style, tone, speed and expression of the reader.

CiLT

CONSTRUCTING SIMPLE SENTENCES

Children can be encouraged to construct their own sentences in a foreign language once they are able to remember short finger rhymes. They can then change known words by substituting their own. A lovely French finger rhyme, which teaches the words for members of the family, can be found in LJR's *Entre dans la ronde*:

> *Bonjour, Papa.*   Talk to thumb
> *Bonjour, Maman.*   To index finger
> *Bonjour, mon frère.*   To middle finger
> *Bonjour, ma sœur.*   To fourth finger
> *Et moi, bonjour petit.*   To little finger.

When children know this confidently, it is possible to teach them how to talk about their own family. Children in KS1 are certainly able to do this, as they count each member of the family on their fingers:

> *Dans ma famille, il y a Papa, Maman et moi.*
> *Dans ma famille, il y a Maman, ma sœur, et moi.*
> *Dans ma famille, il y a Papa, Maman, mon frère Guy, mon frère Marc, ma sœur Mary, mon chien Pippa, et moi.*

Learners can also create their own finger rhyme based closely on the existing structure. How about a finger rhyme to say hello to some of the teachers and learning support assistants?

> *Bonjour, Mademoiselle Barnes.*
> *Bonjour, Mademoiselle Gibbs.*
> *Bonjour, Monsieur Patel.*
> *Bonjour, Madame Williams.*
> *Ça va?*

This activity really empowers children, as they begin to understand that they can manipulate the language and can personalise what they want to say, by slightly changing a well-known pattern. This early feeling of success is an important stage in the learners' language development. The technique can be used again when they are ready to manipulate language in other ways.

Later, when the children are able to read and to copywrite the same finger rhyme, they can write the same brief description of their own family, and also to choose a well-known character to write for, e.g.

> *Je m'appelle Bart Simpson. Dans ma famille, il y a Papa, Maman, ma sœur Lisa, ma sœur Maggie, et moi.*

I can construct simple spoken sentences

I can construct simple written sentences

A German finger rhyme which young children enjoy performing is *Ein großer Hund*, which can be found in the Goethe Institut's *Komm mit!* course:

> *Ein großer Hund*
> *Eine kleine Katze*
> *Da kommt die Maus*
> *Und das Spiel ist aus!*

Encourage the children to replace the words *Hund* and *Katze*. You can provide a bank of possible words for the children to choose from, to avoid difficulties with gender and syllables:

> *Hund – Bär, Fisch*
> *Katze – Spinne, Raupe, Schlange*

This Spanish rhyme is usually played with toes but could be played with fingers, starting with the little one:

> *Éste cerdito encontró un huero,*
> *Éste lo cascó,*
> *Éste le echó la sal,*
> *Éste lo frió,*
> *Y éste gordito se lo comió.*

BUILDING SENTENCES

If children are to develop the ability to form their own sentences, they need to learn about the kinds of words that can be combined to make them. Teachers sometimes say that children can easily learn nouns in a foreign language, but that it seems really difficult to think of interesting and engaging ways to teach them adjectives, verbs or even adverbs. These issues do not need to cause problems. If you can think creatively about active ways in which young children learn, then building up a repertoire of frequently used adjectives, verbs, adverbs and prepositions can be easily achieved.

The Literacy Strategy aims to make learners more aware of the names and functions of different parts of speech, and learning a foreign language can considerably aid this process and bring an interesting dimension into the children's learning.

To begin with, teach the children the names of various types of words in the foreign language as well as in English:

CILT

noun	nom	Nomen	nombre
adjective	adjectif	Adjektiv	adjetivo
verb	verbe	Verb	verbo
pronoun	pronom	Pronomen	pronombre
adverb	adverbe	Adverb	adverbio

Additional words can be taught as necessary, but the above five form a useful set for learners in primary schools. Traditional physical response can be used as a fun and motivating way of simply teaching the children to discriminate between these words. Get the children to respond when you call out one of the above words. The actions can be anything you like, as long as you are consistent, but you could try the following:

Using our arms to speed us up for an **adverb**

Shaking hands for a **conjunction**

Hands on head for a **noun**

Pointing in any direction for a **preposition**

It is also important to teach the children how to recognise the dictionary 'code' for the above terms. What is the 'code' in the set of class dictionaries? It might be as follows:

n.	noun
a.	adjective
v. (but also possibly v.r., v.t., and v.i.)	verb
pron.	pronoun
adv.	adverb

A variation to introduce into this physical response game is initially to hold up text cards, as shown below, with the words shown either in English or in the foreign language, or both. The children can demonstrate their understanding of what is on the card by performing the appropriate physical response.

When the children understand the dictionary 'code' for these terms, allow them to respond to 'code cards' instead:

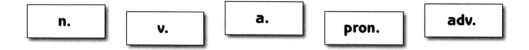

The next stage is to encourage them to respond when you call out a variety of nouns, verbs, and so on, which they must identify by showing the correct physical response. Try at first using some of the high frequency words which the children know well. In the text level chapter, p53, there is a suggestion about how to extend this technique using short pieces of text.

It is important to give children opportunities to use real dictionaries in order to develop their dictionary skills. Working in pairs or individually, they could use a bi-lingual dictionary to find out simple information about certain words, such as their gender. Children should have been introduced to the notion of gender before being asked to find genders in the dictionary. Even in Key Stage 1, children enjoy performing 'sorting and setting' activities with familiar objects such as cuddly toys. They can be asked to separate all the *une* toys from the *un* by placing them on separate mats. Similarly in German, they divide the toys initially into two groups, *ein* and *eine*. Later, they might be able to divide the toys on to three mats, when they recognise the toys by their definite article: *der, die* and *das*.

Working with a list of five nouns, the children could be asked simply to find out the gender of each word and to record it on a chart:

	Type of word	m or f?
glace	n	m
citron	n	
café	n	
vanille	n	
chocolat	n	

In this exercise, the children are told that each word is a noun, and they are only asked to find the gender. However, in order to find the gender of each word, for instance *citron*, they have to look through all of the following information:

citron [sitR͂ɔ] nm *(fruit)* lemon.

First they have to locate the headword *citron* in the dictionary. They then need to know that what follows it, in square brackets, tells us how to pronounce the word, but that at this moment they are not looking for that information. The nm then tells them that this is a noun, and that it is masculine. On this occasion, they are not even asked for the meaning (lemon). It is important that children learn where the information is to be found, and to know what that information means.

Regular practice in dictionary use can be given, using a variety of types of word, and for a variety of purposes. Sometimes the learners can be asked to write down the phonetic transcription of the words, or they can be asked to find the meaning. The alphabet lists in French, German and Spanish (see Appendix 2 on p78) provide some of the high frequency words used in the primary MFL classroom. By scanning the list, you will notice that there is a mixture of nouns, adjectives, adverbs and verbs. If you work with language taken from this list, or from the songs, poems and other material which you already use with the children, you can re-cycle the language they have already learned and use it to teach them more about language.

TEACHING NEW WORDS: NOUNS

Teachers are usually confident about teaching nouns to young learners, but can sometimes find it difficult to teach other types of words, such as verbs, pronouns, adjectives or adverbs. However, we can use interesting and stimulating methodology to teach **all types of words**, involving the use of mime, movement, music, flashcards, realia or a mixture of all of these. It is a good idea to invent a mime to illustrate a word or an idea, so that the children have a physical response which they can give to show comprehension.

In the following example, we will teach four new nouns, but the techniques are transferable to other kinds of words. The methodology outlined here assumes a learning cycle of listening, speaking, reading and writing, but you can best judge when the pupils are ready to focus on aspects of reading or writing.

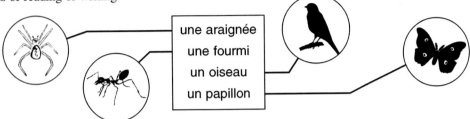

une araignée
une fourmi
un oiseau
un papillon

- Using pictorial flashcards or cuddly toys, say the new word for the children to hear, and encourage them to echo the word back to you. Vary the tone, pitch and dynamics of your voice to add interest, and encourage the children to mimic the style in which you say the word as well as the way you pronounce and enunciate it.

- With the flashcard or cuddly toy clearly visible (so that the meaning of the word is obvious, and English does not need to be used), accompany your speaking with an action which illustrates the word:

  une araignée let one hand 'run' like a spider around your other hand.
  une fourmi   let one finger 'walk' very slowly across the back of your other   hand.
  un oiseau   flap your arms gently at your sides to mimic a bird flying.
  un papillon   cross your hands and wave them in tiny movements.

- Play a physical response game asking the children to respond only with the agreed action when you say one of the four words or, alternatively, when you spell out one of the words.

- Play a verbal response game, performing one action after another at random so that the children call out the correct names.

- Play *Répétez si c'est vrai:* perform an action and say one of the four words. If the word you say matches the action you are performing, the children must also perform the action. If the word you say does not match the action you are performing, the children sit perfectly still and remain silent.

- Perform a *Mexican wave* around the classroom, or sitting in a circle on the carpet. With the children, decide on the word pattern, and perform it around the circle with words and actions. Examples of *Mexican waves* using any of the four words might include:

  une fourmi, une fourmi, une fourmi, une araignée.
  un oiseau, un papillon, un oiseau, un papillon.
  une araignée, un fourmi, un oiseau, un papillon.

  You can make the it more exciting by giving a random signal, such as a handclap, which tells the children that the message must change direction and be passed back the other way around the circle.

CILT

- Play *Pelmanism* (a memory game) using the flashcards, or with picture and text cards together.

- Ask a child to close his eyes. In silence, show the rest of the class which cuddly toy you are putting into a bag. The child opens his eyes, puts his hand into the bag and guesses only by touch which cuddly toy it is.

- Say a word and ask the children to clap the number of syllables.

- Play *Cat and mouse* and similar games in the school hall or playground, but use the selected MFL vocabulary as your signal words.

- Play the *Secret signal game*. Place the four new words into a particular order, using realia or picture or text flashcards (or simply write the four words on the board). Send the 'guesser' out of the room, then in silence choose a 'signaller' who will demonstrate his or her signal to the rest of the class. This signal must be subtle, yet clearly visible by all in the class. The 'guesser' comes back into the classroom. The children all chorus the first word, repeating it rhythmically, until the signal indicates that they move onto the next word. The 'guesser' must try to notice what happens when the children change words, and therefore guess who is the signaller.

- Sequence the words into dictionary order.

TEACHING ADJECTIVES

Many of the techniques described above can be used or adapted for the teaching of adjectives and other kinds of words. Here is a core of adjectives which young children appear to enjoy using. They are listed in alphabetical order by language:

FRENCH			
	épouvantable	noir	
	étrange	orange	
	fantastique	petit	**GERMAN**
abominable	fatigué	rouge	
bizarre	formidable	terrible	
bleu	grand	timide	blau / hässlich
calme	heureux	triste	dick / intelligent
drôle	horrible		dumm / klein
enrhumé	jaune		dünn / riesig
	magnifique		fantastisch / scheu
	minuscule		froh / schön
		SPANISH	furchtbar / schwarz
			gelb / super
			groß / weiß
aburrido	emocionante	fenomenal	perfecto	grün / wunderbar
azul	estupendo	feo	ruidoso	gut
bonito	excelente	horrible	terrible
bueno	fantástico	horroroso	tranquilo
despacio	fatal	maravilloso	triste

Certain adjectives are easy to act out, but all adjectives can be spoken with appropriate body language and vocal expression to make the meaning clear. The action associated with words such as colours can simply be to touch something of that colour as you say the word. All games and activities should be played with this kind of active vocal and bodily expression if possible. If you can find a way of depicting an adjective visually, then many of the activities mentioned above in relation to nouns can be used to teach and practise it. The adjectives can all be expressed pictorially, as these illustrations show:

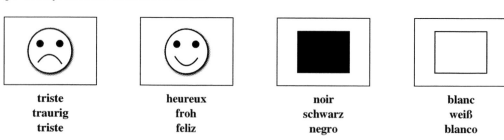

triste	heureux	noir	blanc
traurig	froh	schwarz	weiß
triste	feliz	negro	blanco

When children are given opportunities to act 'in the style of an adjective', they can be very expressive with their voice and physical gestures. Designing *Mexican waves* using adjectives can be great fun, and it certainly seems to reinforce in the mind of the learners that adjectives are descriptive words. For instance, a *Mexican wave* in which the children alternate between sad and happy shows two contrasting moods, with very different facial expressions and tone of voice. This must surely help to consolidate the idea of what adjectives are, and what they mean. Sometimes, very young children are unclear about the exact meaning of an adjective which describes a mood, characteristic or emotion, not because they are unfamiliar with the actual word, but because they have not had any experience of certain emotions or moods; they are then unable to distinguish between one emotion and another. Dramatising the words in this way allows the children to experience a range of feelings through vocal and physical expression.

Initially, the *Mexican waves* can be used as a tool for the children to say the adjective in the style and tone of voice which illustrates its meaning. When a body of adjectives has been confidently mastered in this way, then the vocabulary used in the *Mexican wave* can be anything, but has to be spoken in the style of the adjective. For instance, when the children have learned the days of the week, they can each in turn say a day in the correct sequence, round and round the circle. The teacher can at random call out an adjective in the foreign language, which alters the mood of the *Mexican wave*, making it sad, happy, bored, angry or confused, for example!

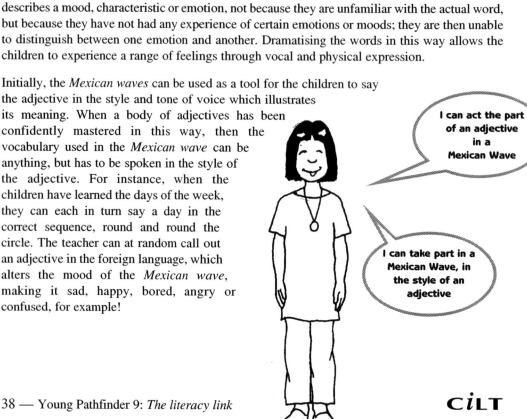

I can act the part of an adjective in a Mexican Wave

I can take part in a Mexican Wave, in the style of an adjective

CiLT

Similarly, you can allow the children to recite some of their favourite rhymes or poems in the 'mood' of an adjective. The poem could be anything which the children know well. In French, a particular favourite is another LJR poem:

> *Toc, toc, toc!*
> *Dring, dring!*
> *Tournez, tournez.*
> *Ouvrez la porte.*
> *Bonjour!*

I can recite a poem in the 'mood' of an adjective

Ask the children for suggestions, in the foreign language as well as in English, as to how the rhyme should be recited. Shall we all be sad, bored, angry, happy or shy? This activity not only provides a context for the children to perform a bank of known poems frequently, but also develops and reinforces an understanding of the function of adjectives in language so that children will know how to use the term adjective appropriately.

USING NOUNS AND ADJECTIVES TOGETHER

In French, all of the adjectives shown in the table on p37 follow the noun, with the exception of *grand* and *petit*, which precede the noun. The idea of the syntax can be constantly reinforced every time you build more complex phrases, by representing the words visually or with visual support,

e.g.   *Un*   *petit*   *écureuil*

Un   *grand*   *serpent*

The phrases which are displayed here pictorially can be 'read' in silence and mimed by the children, or can be read aloud in chorus. Allow the learners to construct phrases using the bank of pictorial flashcards, which then have to be 'read' in some way by the rest of the class. When *petit* and *grand* have become well-established, and the children are used to using them to describe nouns, then other adjectives can be introduced which are placed after the noun:

e.g. Un petit éléphant noir

Un grand papillon triste

Phrases such as these can also be mimed: one finger can denote *un*; *petit* and *grand* can be shown by everyone curling up small or stretching up tall; the animals are usually easy to show, for instance cross over hands and flap gently to show a butterfly or put both hands behind head to model a rabbit's ears; for the adjectives here, point to something blue or show a sad face. The teacher can mime such phrases, which can be 'read' aloud by the class in chorus. As the children gain in confidence, some of them may like to mime a phrase for the rest of the class to 'read' aloud.

I can change the meaning of a sentence by using an adjective

You can allow children to remove one of the adjective-flashcards, and substitute another. For instance, in the last example above, a child may like to remove the sad card, and instead put down the happy card, and notice how it changes the meaning. Initially, with no adjective being used, we can realise that we do not know anything about the butterfly except that it is a butterfly. However, when we use an adjective, we know how the butterfly looks or feels. This activity also helps to reinforce understanding of the function of an adjective in language.

Further activities which can be tried out when the children know a bank of nouns and adjectives are:

- Teacher chooses a noun and an adjective to say together. Pupils respond by miming the chosen phrase.

- Reverse roles, so that the teacher mimes, and pupils have to choose the words (and correct syntax) to describe what they see.

- In pairs or groups of three, children can choose a noun and one or two adjectives which they can mime to the class. The class must guess the foreign language words.

- Perform *Mexican waves* of many types, for example those which involve children memorising an aural pattern and then representing it visually or physically, and those which involve children in speaking and performing actions.

CILT

- Pupils can use ICT to invent their own combinations to make posters. They can choose a phrase which combines a noun and an adjective (or more than one adjective), and import clipart to illustrate.

- Printed off, these can be used in a game so that other pupils guess what the phrase is to match the illustrations.

- When completed, these can be e-mailed to a partner class abroad, who have been working on the same aspect in their English lessons and who will e-mail their English versions to your class. Copies of both sets can then make a wall display for discussion and provide an ideal opportunity for comparison between English and the foreign language.

It is important for the teacher always to model structures using the correct syntax. When visual support is given, it encourages the children to use the displayed syntax, without even making comparisons with English initially.

In German, you can use nouns and adjectives together with very young learners, but at this stage it is best to avoid the issue of agreement when the adjective precedes the noun. A simple structure as in the examples below is still easy to display visually:

Der Schmetterling ist scheu.   *Die Katze ist unartig.*   *Das Eichhörnchen ist müde.*

The verb *ist* can simply be a flashcard showing the word as text. The same procedures can be followed as suggested in the French examples above.

When you wish to use a different syntactical pattern with the pupils, it is be advisable to select groups of nouns by gender so that one pattern at a time is followed:

Das ist ...

Masculine	Feminine	Neuter
ein brauner Bär	*eine scheue Schlange*	*ein braunes Eichhörnchen*
ein fantastischer Fisch	*eine intelligente Kuh*	*ein schönes Schwein*

In Spanish, too, you need to be careful with adjectival endings and therefore you may like to try grouping the words as you introduce them. For instance, you need to make sure that adjectives ending in –o agree with the noun, such as:

Masculine	Feminine
un gato tranquilo	*una tortuga tranquila*
un conejo perfecto	*una jirafa perfecta*

I can describe people and objects using adjectives

Many adjectives in Spanish however end in –e and this does not change according to gender:

Masculine	Feminine
un rinoceronte enorme	*una serpiente enorme*
un periquito verde	*una vaca verde*

In French, special attention must be paid to any changes in pronunciation which result when nouns beginning with a vowel sound are chosen to follow *grand* or *petit*. For instance:

un grand écureuil/ un petit écureuil
un grand éléphant/ un petit éléphant

This concept can be easily explained to pupils by showing them the words and asking them to work out why this might be happening. It is an opportunity to discuss vowels and vowel sounds, and similarities and differences with English can be explored.

Similarly, some adjectival endings **sound** different when they are feminine. Ask the children if they can identify what **sounds** different, before showing them that the words also **look** different.

Only some of the French adjectives in regular use in the primary classroom will sound different:

blanc	▷	*blanche*
content		*contente*
vert		*verte*
sérieux		*sérieuse*
heureux		*heureuse*

Discussion may lead the pupils to the discovery that the final consonant is hardly ever pronounced in French words, and that the feminine ending means that the preceding consonants are no longer final.

Most of the French adjectives in the table on p37 have the advantage of not **sounding** different when describing a feminine noun, so the teacher can embark upon speaking and listening activities which group together nouns and adjectives without having to deal with this issue. When the pupils begin to write simple captions to describe nouns and adjectives, the teacher can restrict the bank of words from which pupils can select.

With opportunities to practise such activities on a regular basis, the pupils will become very aware of which words are nouns and which are adjectives. A physical response game can be played in the playground or hall as a warm-up in P.E. Call out a range of words from the known bank of nouns and adjectives and get the pupils to choose which of two actions to perform, according to whether they think they are hearing a noun or an adjective. For the purposes of a game like this, agree with the children that the colours will all be adjectives rather than nouns. The actions chosen can be any which are different and easily performed, e.g.

CiLT

Noun	*Adjective*
Stand up	Sit down
Run to the window	Run to the door
Hop on one foot	Swing arms in the air
Hands on head	Wave one hand in the air

The game can be played as an elimination game if you wish, but does not need to be. It can also be played in the classroom for a couple of minutes at a time if the agreed actions do not require movement or too much space.

Similarly, a sorting activity can be regularly performed using a selection of flashcards and realia and two mats or containers on to which the items are placed. When an object or flashcard is selected, the teacher asks a pupil whether it is a noun or an adjective and the pupil then places it on the appropriate mat. Here is what your two mats might look like:

When this sorting activity has been completed, it can in turn provide a stimulus for making phrases linking nouns and adjectives together.

TEACHING VERBS

Certain verbs are very easy to mime or to associate with a physical action, and also to illustrate pictorially, and these verbs can be used to teach and reinforce the concept of what a verb is and what a verb does. On the following page are some examples using the third person singular.

If our initial intention is to help learners to **identify** verbs in the foreign language and to **use** them, it does not matter that we are restricting them in a particular activity to using verbs only in the third person. By using third person singular verbs in this context, we can expand on the activities already developed using nouns and adjectives.

French	German	Spanish
chante	singt	canta
danse	tanzt	baila
ronfle	schnurrt	ronca
nage	schwimmt	nada
court	rennt	corre
dort	schläft	duerme
mange	isst	come
écrit	schreibt	escribe
lit	liest	lee

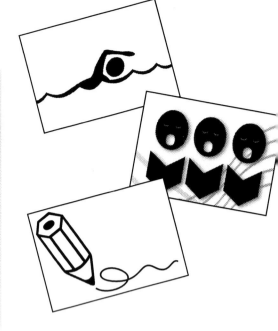

We can play the same responding activities as we did earlier with nouns and adjectives, but initially only to practise the verbs. Children can respond:

- to a spoken word with a mime;
- to a spoken word, pointing to a picture flashcard or a text flashcard;
- to a teacher mime with a spoken response;
- to a teacher mime, pointing to a picture flashcard or a text flashcard;
- to a text flashcard with a mime;
- by matching a text flashcard to a picture, or miming to a text flashcard;
- by means of a non-verbal physical response game in the hall or playground.

When you feel that the pupils know the verbs really well, integrate them into your general sentence level work so that you are now working with nouns, adjectives and verbs. You can now make sentences such as …

Un petit serpent jaune danse.
Une grande vache contente chante.

Ein kleiner, schöner Hund schwimmt.
Eine grosse, dicke Schildkröte singt.

Una cabra bonita y blanca corre.
Un toro chiquitín y negro baila.

Again, it is important to allow the children to perform the sorting activities regularly and frequently. From now on you will need three mats or containers for the words! You can also extend the physical response game which identifies nouns, adjectives and verbs.

ciLT

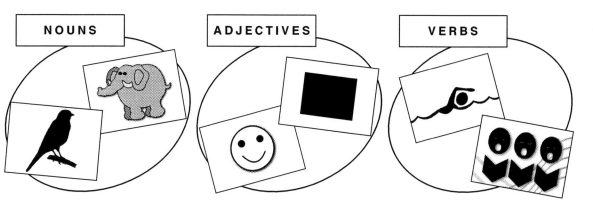

| NOUNS | ADJECTIVES | VERBS |

Now that the learners are able to identify and manipulate verbs, they will be able to form complete sentences of their own in the foreign language, and will notice that sentences cannot make sense without verbs. Allow the children to play games in which they change the verbs in the sentence, in order to change the meaning. They can make some very funny, nonsensical sentences with the words given as examples in this chapter.

> I can make different sentences using verbs which I know

 ## TEACHING ADVERBS

Here is a core of adverbs which young children love using:

FRENCH	GERMAN	SPANISH
doucement	leise	suavemente
fort	laut	fuerte
lentement	langsam	despacio
vite	schnell	rápido
ensemble	zusammen	juntos
seul	allein	solo

The 'illustration' for each of these could be as follows: *doucement* is always spoken quietly, *fort* is always spoken loudly, *lentement* is spoken slowly, and *vite* quickly; *ensemble* is always spoken when you are standing or sitting with someone else, and *seul* is always uttered when you are standing alone.

These can also be incorporated into the non-verbal physical response game:

doucement	'Shh!' gesture
fort	hands over ears, or similar 'loud' gesture
lentement	slow-motion walking
vite	running
ensemble	everyone stand together, or stand in small groups
seul	everyone stand alone

The adverbs can also be incorporated into the physical response game in which children differentiate between parts of speech. You will now need to choose four actions, so that the children can show a response to nouns, adjectives, verbs and adverbs!

Once the pupils are used to dealing regularly with nouns, adjectives and verbs, you can easily add adverbs into your sentences.

You can now perform a similar activity in the classroom. Show the children a mime or a pictorial sentence, and say the sentence aloud. **One element** in the sentence must be incorrect, e.g.

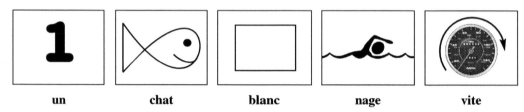

un	**chat**	**blanc**	**nage**	**vite**

The incorrect element here is that we have displayed or mimed *fish*, but we have said *cat*. Ask the children to tell you which words is wrong, and also which kind of word it is. This will help the children to identify the different elements in the sentence.

JUMBLED SENTENCES

To take this activity a stage further, you can organise a carousel of group work. Form six or seven small groups, either at tables or using a larger space such as the hall. Give each group a sheet of paper for recording their work. On each table place a set of six flashcards, similar to those shown in the example above, but a different set for each table. The flashcards must be completely jumbled up. Allow each group a certain time limit, within which they must try to work out what the sentence could be by placing the flashcards in the correct syntactical order. They must also write down their sentence (in secret!) on their sheet of paper. At the end of the time limit, each group must jumble up the flashcards on their table, then move to the next table and repeat the activity with the next set of flashcards. This might seem like a noisy activity, but in fact the children are very eager not to be overheard by other groups, so they work very quietly and usually whisper the words or move the flashcards around in silence and nod to

I can re-organise a jumbled sentence so that it makes sense

c*i*LT

each other. In fact, you could make it a rule of the game that it must be played in total silence, using only gestures to move and point to flashcards. This activity allows the children to form and to re-read simple sentences, recognising whether or not they make sense. It prepares them for later opportunities to write their own simple sentences. Much fun is had when the 'Quiz sheets' are marked at the end of the activity!

The *Jumbled sentences* game can be played frequently, and progression can be built in throughout the primary phase. When the children are able to read text in the foreign language, the game can be played using text flashcards, and also flashcards which feature punctuation. Practice can be given in re-assembling both statements and questions, e.g.

?	tu	-	appelles	t'	Comment

The children will enjoy building up their writing and recording skills gradually by writing their own sentences and illustrating them. The posters which they create can now display more sophisticated use of language.

Using a software package such as *Storybook weaver,* children can make their own storybooks by creating the text, selecting a graphic background for the illustrations and importing a very wide range of people, characters and objects. Such an opportunity also makes it possible for children to show what they can do, at different levels.

The children could choose a question and answer which they know well, for example 'What is your name?' 'My name is ...' They could scan in a photograph of themselves, or take a photo using a digital camera, and create a poster by importing the picture, and using a callout (speech bubble) to say their name and then ask the name of the next person. These posters than be displayed around the room in the style of a *Mexican wave*:

If similar posters are created by the partner class abroad, they can be intermingled within the display to create an impression of friendship and communication between the two sets of children.

3. Text level

Text level work focuses on comprehension and composition of language. It is vital that children develop confidence when faced with extended pieces of language, either in aural form (listening to a story, poem or song) or as a visual text (a letter, a storybook, an e-mail, or other form of written language). Children must be given opportunities to encounter a variety of text, and to enjoy it and cope with it confidently.

There are many exciting and interesting sources of text available; these can be found in fiction and non-fiction books, magazines, comics, anthologies, audio and video resources, CD-ROM software and the Internet. It is impossible to recommend a list of ideal book titles, as there are so many, both at home and abroad, that it must be left to the teacher's judgement as to what might best stimulate the interest of the pupils at each stage in their literacy and MFL development.

The many kinds of resources referred to here provide a wealth of variety and media, and bring richness and interest into the classroom. Using the Internet and ICT as a resource has enormous benefits which go beyond simply the provision of diverse and interesting text. It brings with it a cultural dimension; it allows children to enter foreign countries and to experience the world of others in a very immediate way, and to bring visitors from abroad straight into the classroom. The foreign country can become an immediate reality, and might cease to be something which is beyond the experience and imagination of some children.

INVOLVING THE LEARNER IN THE TEXT

The teacher must always have a clear idea of what the children are required to do when text level work is being tackled, in other words what the aims and objectives of each text level activity are. It is important that the teacher does not expect the children to understand every text completely. Asking the children the **meaning** of particular words and phrases which they hear and see is not always the best approach, as this is a very difficult task and some children are unlikey to succeed in this. There are many other purposes for working at text level, other than understanding the meaning of individual words or phrases. A significant advantage of storytelling is that it allows the children **exposure to the foreign language**.

When working at text level it is important to allow the children to feel involved, and to make it clear to them on what level they are expected to be involved. The children can be invited to listen only, to listen and to read by following the text, to read aloud, to follow a text and to join in with a repetitive phrase or chorus, or to listen for and respond to key words and features using mime or manipulating text.

Children can listen to and read extended pieces of foreign language for a variety of purposes:

- to experience how the language sounds when spoken at pace;
- to experience the **style** of storytelling, including the use of different voices for different characters;

- for gist;
- to respond to key words and phrases;
- to respond to features of the text;
- for meaning;
- to develop concentration skills;
- to experience listening to and reading text which is beyong their level of active performance/ more difficult than they are able to produce themselves/ as a model of the language;
- to read aloud in order to help develop fluency, and to provide a context for phoneme/ grapheme correspondences.

The teacher must decide which of these objectives is being met when selecting text level activities.

Short pieces of text can be used to allow the children to listen for particular sounds in the text, in other words to reinforce some word level work. The following text contains many examples of the phoneme [ɛ̃], which can be represented by the grapheme *in*. (There are no examples in this text of *ain* or *ein*, although these are of course also possible graphemes for this phoneme.)

in (un)

Le lutin du moulin

Ce matin dans un jardin,
un petit robot malin
est assis sur le chemin,
est assis près du moulin.

Qui lui fait un gros câlin ?
C'est le lutin du moulin !

Ce matin dans un jardin,
un joli petit lapin
est assis sur le chemin,
est assis près du sapin.

Qui lui fait un gros câlin ?
C'est le lutin du moulin !

Remplacez lapin, par poussin, pantin, etc.

Rocard A, Je veux lire
avec Ludo bleu
(Hachette, 1996)

Firstly, model the text for the children to allow them to hear what it sounds like whilst they follow the text. When the children are used to the sound of it, allow them to notice how the phoneme [ɛ̃] is represented, and allow them to point to these graphemes in the text.

On subsequent readings, allow the children to respond each time they hear the phoneme [ɛ̃] in any of the following ways:

- make a physical sign, e.g. wave a hand in the air;
- swap seats with their neighbour;
- take a piece of multilink or lego, adding a piece each time the phoneme is heard. These pieces can be counted at the end of the reading (this can be done in small groups);
- pass an object, such as a cuddly toy, to the next person in the line or circle, and see how far the toy has travelled by the end of the poem;
- allow a child, or more than one child, to travel across the room during the reading of the text, by taking one pace each time the phoneme is heard. Ask the class to predict where the child's journey will finish. The class will also monitor the journey, to check that steps are only taken when the phoneme is uttered.

The above activities offer a variety of possible responses, in order to maintain interest, while using the same text on numerous occasions. You can encourage the children gradually to join in with reading the text aloud, once it becomes very familiar by ear to them. We can use extended texts to invite children to read aloud both in chorus and independently, so that they have the opportunity to speak with fluency, rhythm, pace and interest.

Activities using text flashcards are useful in developing knowledge of phoneme/grapheme correspondences further. Make flashcards of certain words, selected from the text, and rehearse the children in recognising these words. As you show each flashcard, tell them what the card says and encourage them to echo the word. Then distribute the cards among the children, who can have one card each or one between two. Now read the text aloud to them, asking all of them to echo the word they are holding whenever they hear it in the text, and to hold up their card. The children can then pass their card along to the next person in the circle, and the activity repeated with the children responding to a different word.

It is certainly true to say that children do not mind listening to a story for purposes other than that of understanding the meaning of the words. Although meaning is important, and might sometimes be the main focus of a storytelling session, it need not always feature highly. Therefore, when you are selecting a range of stories for children to hear, do not be put off if a story has some difficult words or phrases. If the story has enough other features to hold the learners' attention, they will still enjoy listening to it and will benefit from doing so.

LISTENING TO STORIES

This element of text level work contributes greatly to young learners' language development, as it provides opportunities to hear extended pieces of language within a familiar and meaningful context. If children are involved in storytelling activities on a regular basis, it can build up their confidence as learners of a foreign language, as they come to realise that they can understand the **story** without needing to understand **every word** of the story.

Children often enjoy particular stories so much that they choose to hear them again and again. It has been the experience of many parents to have to read a favourite bed-time story as often as possible. When doing so it is clear that the child has a strong emotional attachment to the story and that it is not necessarily the **meaning** of the story that the child is attracted by; his or her imagination is stimulated by the conjuring up of images which portray the story, and the **sounds** of particular words and phrases, often repeated as a chorus throughout the story, are tantalisingly comforting in their ever-increasing familiarity.

When children first start to enjoy English stories in this way, it can be noticed that the language and concepts in the story are initially beyond their level of understanding. Nevertheless, they are captivated by the **structure** and **shape** of the tale, the **sound of the voices**, the **rhythm** and **repetition** of little-understood phrases. It may be much later in the young learners' development when they can fully understand the actual meaning of the story. Storytelling takes the children's imagination and their knowledge of language to a higher level. If we only read stories to children which they could easily understand at their level of conceptual and linguistic development, there would be little to hold their attention.

There are a great many phrases which form the repertoire of storytelling language in English. In the early stages of storytelling, these might be: *Once upon a time …; Fee – fi – fo –fum!; … and they lived happily ever after*; etc. How many of us, as adults, can still remember these phrases, which were deeply imprinted in our memories from the earliest times? And can we still hear the intonation, pitch, dynamics and vocal expression with which they were uttered?

It has been our experience when telling **foreign-language stories** to young learners that the same linguistic and imaginative development can take place. The children usually listen with great concentration, and become fully involved in repeating or chorusing words and phrases which arise regularly in the text.

Children will listen with intense interest and great pleasure to stories, and will gradually remember the key words and phrases as if they are remembering a musical phrase. The children seem to enjoy the story for its **sound** and its **expression.**

It is often a good idea to read stories in the foreign language which are already well known to the children. Obvious examples are traditional tales such as *Little Red Riding Hood, The three little pigs, Goldilocks* and *Hansel and Gretel*, and more recent stories such as *The very hungry caterpillar*.

Here is an example, in German, of a story with a repeating chorus: *Sieben im Bett* by Petra Probst. The structure of the story is simple, as it tells how seven children are pushed out of bed, one at a time, by the cuddly toys who want to take their places. The story itself can therefore be easily understood by the listener, as the illustrations are clear, colourful, amusing and engaging. I have found that within the first two or three pages the children want to join in with the repetitive phrases. Each animal in turn calls out *'Macht mal Platz!'* and then jumps on to the bed *und tat*

einen Satz. The children are certainly helped by the rhyme of *Platz* and *Satz,* and the rhythm of the phrase. Whenever an animal jumps on to the bed and a child falls on to the floor, the children chorus '*Plumps-pardauz, eins fiel raus*'.

We have read this story to children in Year 2 who already were already learning German, and also to children from Year 2 to Year 6 who were not learning German, but French, and we found that both groups enjoyed it and joined in with the text with equal enthusiasm and engagement. At no point did any of the young listeners feel that they could not understand the story because they did not know the meaning of particular words. In fact, the story was requested time and again by the children, who certainly appeared to enjoy the story for its sound and structure, and who were able to participate actively in the telling of it.

> I can follow a story and join in the chorus

A story with repetitive phrases in French is *Le petit chat perdu*. The little cat is hungry, but does not know how to ask for milk. In turn, each animal in the farmyard tries to offer advice when the little cat says '*j'ai faim!*', but the little cat says she would not like their food and says to all of them '*Je veux du lait!*' Children listening to this story can join in immediately with '*J'ai faim!*' and '*Je veux du lait!*', and over a period of time they are also able to join in with all the other animal noises!

Children need to hear a wide variety of stories on a regular basis in order to become as familiar with storybook language in the foreign language as they are in English. When they are familiar with a bank of favourite stories, many children will be able to select the key elements such as *Il était une fois* ...and to recite these elements from memory. If shown the text of these key elements on flashcards, some children will also be able to sequence them in the correct order, or to pick them out from the main body of the text.

> I can listen to stories and recognise key elements

> I can listen to and enjoy a variety of stories

It is possible to read a story to quite young children, in which the level of language is far too sophisticated for them to understand. However, by asking the children to listen out for and to respond to key words and phrases, they can be actively involved in the story, listening for individual words and phrases, and yet be exposed to a highly sophisticated and extended piece of language. An example of such a story is *The rainbowfish* by Marcus Pfister. Many children will already know this story in English, but it has been translated into many other languages. (*Arc-en-ciel, le plus beau poisson des océans; Der Regenbogenfisch*). The illustrations in the *Rainbowfish* books are very appealing and help to captivate the children while they are listening to the story.

You can select one key word or phrase which the children must listen out for and respond to the first time the story is read to them. On subsequent readings, new words or phrases can be added to involve the listeners even more in the particular language of the story. Children could respond to the following words and phrases ….

Whenever the children hear …	They respond by …
Arc-en-ciel or *Regenbogenfisch* (the name of the Rainbowfish)	Raising their arms above their head, drawing a rainbow shape in the air, and repeating the name of the fish.
écailles or *Glitzerschuppen*	They stroke their arms, in silence, to show off their beautiful glittery scales.
poisson or *Fisch*	They mime, in silence, an agreed action to look like a fish.

You can extend this list as the story becomes ever more familiar to the children in the foreign language so that they become involved in extended listening practice.

Reading stories and big books provides learners with the opportunity to **see** extended pieces of text and for some close sentence level or word level work. If big books in the foreign language are not easily available to the teacher, there are alternatives: big books which the teacher already has in English could be used, with simple foreign language text placed over the top of the English using 'post-its' or similar. Alternatively, text and pictures can be easily displayed using an overhead projector.

Children can be encouraged to find particular words or phrases in the text, either by listening or by reading. This could be introduced by using a story which the children are used to **hearing** in the foreign language. For instance, when they are familiar with the *Rainbowfish* story in the foreign language, their reading skills can be developed by letting them follow the text with you as you read it aloud. Initially they continue to respond with the actions which you have used to involve them in listening to the story, but increasingly they can respond by holding up text flashcards with matching key words.

Some children will be able to find the key words and phrases in the text of the big book. If an interactive whiteboard is available in the classroom, sections of the text being read can be displayed on the screen and the children can circle key words with their finger. Younger children may be able to use an electronic notepad which is linked to the digital whiteboard. Every time a key word or phrase is heard, a child can circle it or copywrite it on the electronic notepad, the results of which can be seen by the whole class on the whiteboard.

Here are some examples of words or phrases which are particular to their own language, and which children appear to enjoy and remember:

Red Riding Hood
Goldilocks
Cinderella
the wolf
the wicked witch
the princess
the king
abracadabra
One, two, three ...
And they lived
happily ever
after.

le petit chaperon rouge
un, deux, trois ...
le roi
la reine
la princesse
le loup
la sorcière
Hansel et Gretel
Cendrillon

Rotkäppchen
die alte, böse Hexe
eins, zwei, drei ...
Hänsel und Gretel
der König
die Königin
die Prinzessin
Es war einmal ...
der Wolf

I can find
der König
in a story
text

Caperucita Roja
Ricitos de oro
Cenicienta
el lobo
la bruja

la princesa
Era una vez un
príncipe que ...
Había una vez ...
un rey
una rana

... y vivieron
felíces y
comieron
perdices.
...y colorín
colorado, este
cuento se ha
acabado.

There are also stories whose language has been re-worked especially for children in the foreign language classroom. There are some lovely story activities for young learners in KS 1, using French and English, in *Entre dans la ronde* (LJR). In *La boîte magique* and *L'étoile magique* the story structure is in English, with key elements given in French. Similarly, for older learners LJR have produced French storytelling packs using language and structures which children seem to find easy to remember. The story is available as a sequence of pictures which can be copied on to flashcards or overhead transparencies. This allows the teacher to tell the story while making the meaning explicit to the children through the use of pictures. Text can be introduced as already described, using flashcards or transparencies, and can be matched up to the pictures and placed in correct sequential order.

The *French storytelling resource pack* by Daniel Tierney and Fay Humphreys includes pictures and exciting methodology for the telling of familiar tales in French and is very motivating for children in Key Stage 2.

CiLT

Additionally, there are two packs of *Petites histoires* in French produced by LJR. In the *Joyeux Noël* pack (LJR) there are several stories on a Christmas theme, including the nativity story, which children find relatively easy to learn by heart and to re-tell. These can provide material for children to perform at an assembly or a concert for parents.

A different kind of story to use with young learners is one in which there is a small body of words and phrases, which are repeated and added to throughout the story. *Die Farben* by Fredrik Vahle and Helme Heine is a lovely German text which children can enjoy when they have learnt the colours *blau, grau, rot,* and *gelb*. A colour is featured within a phrase on each page, and this phrase is then repeated on the next page together with a new phrase containing a different colour word.

Each phrase of the story is very memorable to the listeners. As children become more and more familiar with the text, you will be able to leave out the final word from each line of the story and find that the children will provide the missing word. Although these words are sometimes the colours, which the children know, they children can also draw on their knowledge of **rhyme** in order to find the required word.

The text of the story begins ...

I can recite
a short story
or a poem
from memory

> *Vom Himmel das Blau,*
> *von den Mäusen das Grau,*
> *von Tomaten das Rot*
> *und das Braune vom Brot, ...*

A story with a structure such as this, which repeats phrases and uses rhyme and rhythm in an appealing way, can become a familiar friend to children who will want to listen to it again and again. It is a story which is easily learned by heart, and it will give learners a tremendous feeling of success if they can recite the story from memory.

I can read
aloud a
short story
or poem

It is also very important to give children regular opportunities to read familiar stories aloud from text. When a story becomes very familiar to them by ear, they will make connections between sound and print if they are able to read at normal pace from the storybook itself. This can also help to build the confidence of learners who do not perceive themselves to be 'good readers', and who may lack the confidence to read aloud something similar in English. You can encourage all children to participate in reading aloud together if the text is large enough and clearly visible to all, and when children are confident enough to participate with the group you can invite small groups and then individal children to read aloud.

When you show the text to the children, you can ask them to identify particular words, such as the colours, and also to identify the rhyming words. When playing a *Find the missing words game* with the class, you can give them the opportunity, in a non-threatening way, to look more closely at the text. Display the text as follows:

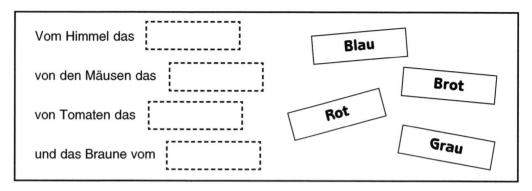

Ask the children if they can remember which words would complete each line of the story and then, if they can find the correct flaschard, to put it into the gap. You can also invite them to put wrong flashcards into the gaps, in order to invent a 'silly story', and then ask the class (or individual children) to read it aloud. A variation on this is to ask all the children to close their eyes, while you move the words around, then invite them to read the story aloud. This activity gives the children the opportunity to read aloud from familiar text, but also to deal in a small way with the unexpected. This can be developed further by putting in words from a completely different context. See if the children can cope with reading the story aloud.

Through shared reading you can provide learners with opportunities to recognise printed words in a variety of settings. Sometimes the children may be able to find particular words within direct speech, such as in a speech bubble or in speech marks. They may also be able to pick out from a text groups of particular words, such as colours, numbers, days of the week, fruit or people's names.

RE-CREATING STORIES

A further opportunity for working with and manipulating text can be provided by cutting up the text into sections and giving a set of the text cards to small groups. You can invite each group to re-build the text by placing the cards in the correct order. This activity can easily be differentiated for varying abilities within the class, and also at different stages in the development of the children, by cutting up the text into longer or shorter chunks. It is much more difficult for children to re-constitute a text word by word than if the text is given line by line. In the example from '*Die Farben*', the most difficult exercise would be to present a group of children with each word on a separate card.

You can also set up a group carousel activity like the *Jumbled sentences* activity described on p46. Divide the class into groups and sit each group together at a table. Present each group with the text of a well-known story which has been cut up into sections. Allow the groups time to reconstitute the story and to see if it makes sense. When they are happy that they have reassembled the text correctly, allow them to glue the pieces of text in the correct order on to a sheet of paper and, if you wish, combine it with pictures. This activity can be done first by the whole class, using pieces of text on the overhead projector, or text cards held by magnets or blu-tack on the whiteboard, or even displayed as sections of text on a digital interactive whiteboard.

If you then want the children to work individually at this activity, after having practised in a group, allow them to create their own version of the story by making their own storybook from a sheet of paper. They can either stick in the storytext in the right order, or copywrite it following the group work, perhaps matching the text with a series of pictures. Alternatively, each child can re-constitute the story using ICT. Without having to write the text themselves, they can manipulate sections of text which have been stored on disk, and place them in the correct sequential order.

This activity can be differentiated according to the ability and developmental stage of individual pupils. For instance, children can re-create a story in the style of *The very hungry caterpillar* by Eric Carle. Some will be able to write simple labels to match pictures, possibly a day of the week on each page or the name of the piece of food eaten by the caterpillar. Other children will be able to do more and label both the day and the food, or they will have progressed further and be able to write short phrases or sentences to match the text. Some will need support from the teacher, some will be able to copywrite by themselves, and others will be able to write certain phrases accurately from memory. Whatever the children can achieve in this respect deserves recognition and praise, and an acknowledgement of what they are able to do in positive terms:

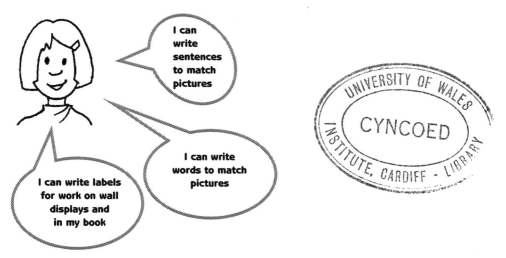

Pupils will also benefit from creating their own stories, possibly modelling them on stories which they know well. Stories involving patterns and sequences, such as *The very hungry caterpillar*, often provide children with the inspiration to create their own story, such as *The very hungry dinosaur/crocodile/spider/zebra*, etc. The children can draw on aspects of the foreign language text and use these as a model for telling their own tale. In creating their own storybooks children can learn about basic text conventions, such as the cover of the book, the author's name, the title and the layout. The storybooks can be read by other children in the class, and even exchanged with partner classes abroad, so that a large bank of reading material is created.

Some children may also enjoy the experience of recording their story on to audio-cassette, with the help of the foreign language assistant, or of having it recorded onto cassette by a child in the partner class abroad. These tapes can then, in turn, feed into the class reading bank for independent listening and reading, and children will engage with this bank of material much more if they have some ownership of it.

Children can draw on their ever-growing knowledge of adjectives, as described in Chapter 2, to build profiles of characters in their stories. In time, they will be able to describe their characteristics, appearance and behaviour.

USING DICTIONARIES

In Chapter 1 opportunities for creating class and individual dictionaries were discussed. If children are accustomed from an early age to using dictionaries, they will find that a dictionary can be a valuable tool with which to achieve what they want to do in their own writing. In Chapters 1 and 2 techniques were described which help learners to understand the alphabetical order and organisation of a dictionary. Text level work of many kinds, such as shared and independent reading and writing, will allow the children to use bi-lingual dictionaries for two purposes, that is to find the spelling and/or discover the meaning of words.

If we look at the dictionary entries for various types of word we see that there is a lot of information given in each entry which children need to understand:

noun	**citron** [sitR̃ɔ̃] nm (*fruit*) lemon
verb	
adjective	
pronoun	
adverb	

As we have already explored in earlier chapters, children need to be given many opportunities to develop their alphabetic knowledge sufficiently well in order to actually locate the headword in the dictionary. They then need to know that what follows the headword, usually in square brackets, is the phonetic transcription of the word which tells us how to pronounce it. After that the dictionary 'code' tells us what kind of word it is. This information is very important, as sometimes words can exist in more than one form. Finally, we are given the meaning of the word, or several possible meanings. When children are working and thinking at text level, they can make decisions about context which allow them to choose the most appropriate meaning from what they find in the dictionary.

The worksheet shown on p60 illustrates how a song text can be used as a stimulus for some dictionary work. The sheet gives the pupils the opportunity to use the dictionary in order to find certain information about the words in a song which they know well. The chosen song is *Quand j'étais bébé petit* by Henri Dès. After getting the children to listen once again closely to the song, give them a short aural and reading sequencing activity in which they place a number from 1 to 5 beside each phrase to denote the order in the phrases heard in the song.

For the dictionary work, some key words have been taken from the song and put into a grid which shows the headword, the phonetic transcription, the type of word, and the meaning. The children must use a dictionary to find the missing information and complete the grid. Some information has already been put into the grid for guidance. Notice that some of the words have been given in English, and others in the foreign language, in order to give the children a reason to use both sections of the bi-lingual dictionary. This work can be done by some children individually, and by others in pairs and small groups, depending on how confident they are in using a dictionary on their own. You can devise much simpler dictionary work, but this type of exercise allows the children to practise using the dictionary in a focused way so that, when they need the dictionary to support independent reading or writing work, they will be more confident and more accurate in their use of it.

I can use a bi-lingual dictionary to check the spelling of words

I can use a bi-lingual dictionary to check the meaning of words

Quand j'étais bébé petit

Quand j'étais bébé petit ,
tout petit tout petit
Que j'faisais pipi popo ailleurs
que dans mon pot
Que j'étalais ma purée partout sur la télé
Que j'tirais les poils du chien
sans qu'il ne dise rien

Quand j'étais bébé petit, tout petit tout petit
Que j'versais mon cacao sur les touches du piano
Que j'mettais des petits poix dans la poche à papa
Que j'laissais tomber les clés au fond des cabinets

Quand j'étais bébé petit, tout petit tout petit
Que j'me balladais tout nu devant des inconnus
Que j'me trainais dans la boue
parce que c'était plus doux
Que j'pleurais en pleine nuit
pour vous tirer du lit

Quand j'étais bébé petit, tout petit tout petit
Que vous m'embrassiez beaucoup
malgré tout malgré tout
Que j'aimerais bien quelquefois
retrouver ce temps là
J'étais si bien contre vous quand j'avais peur du loup

Quand j'étais bébé petit, tout petit tout petit
Petit tout petit tout petit, petit tout petit.

Henri Dès

◁ T E X T E   E X E R C I C E S
▽

1

Numérote les phrases 1 – 2 – 3 – 4 – 5
dans l'ordre que tu les entends dans la
chanson:

☐ Que j'faisais pipi popo
ailleurs que dans mon pot

☐ Que j'mettais des petits pois
dans la poche à papa

☐ Que j'mettais du cacao
sur les touches du piano

☐ Que vous m'embrassiez beaucoup
malgré tout, malgré tout

☐ Que j'tirais les poils du chien
sans qu'il ne dise rien

2

Cherche dans le dictionnaire,
et remplis la grille:

Headword	Pronunciation	Type of word	Meaning
tu		pron	
il			
tirer		v	
boue			
		nm	bed
mettre			
petit		a	
			to cry
quelquefois			
			to pour

CILT

MAKING SENSE OF TEXT

Children need to develop confidence in understanding text, at least on the level of understanding a sequence of events. They can develop this confidence without needing to undertand the meaning of each individual word in a text.

Practice in the sequencing of events does not always need to be performed using a story; the text could be a song text or poem which the children are familiar with. They enjoy learning and performing songs in the foreign language. Why not let them see text, or key words from the text? Then, in small groups, you can present them with a listening puzzle in the style of a jig-saw.

It is useful to build up learners' confidence in this technique gradually. With very young children, ask them to listen to a poem or song, and listen just for two words or ideas. At the end of the poem or song, ask them in which order they heard those words or ideas. Going back to the poem *Marylène la baleine* on p9 of Chapter 1, we could use this now to give the children practice in sequencing events. Ask them to tell you in which order the words *haleine* and *marraine* appear in the text. Let them listen to the poem, and at the end they can tell you verbally, or point to flaschards.

Similarly, we can use the Henri Dès song *Ma forêt* (p24) to simply sequence some of the key words in the order in which we think they appear in the text, using either the text or the picture flashcards.

The songs of Henri Dès, Detlev Jöcker and Rosa Léon, mentioned in the word level chapter, are once again ideal for this exercise. Many of the shorter rhymes, poems and songs which the children know can also be used in this way.

This *Henri Dès* song, *les fleurs nouvelles*, is a favourite of many children:

> *J'aime bien les fleurs nouvelles.*
> *Quand elles sont en bouton.*
> *Faut les regarder longtemps.*
> *Car elles s'ouvrent lentement.*

Before children perform this listening and reading jigsaw puzzle for the first time, they should have had the opportunity to hear the song many times over a long period. In Chapter 1 reference is made to using songs such as this for passive listening to the foreign language, and examples are given of when such opportunities might arise.

The first time you present the children with the puzzle, cut up the song into its four lines, so that all you are asking the children to do is to sequence the four lines in the order in which they are heard in the song. This could be done as a whole-class activity, with each line written on a differently-coloured card and displayed on the board, so that the children can identify the sequence by saying *rouge, bleu, blanc, jaune*.

I can put a story, song or poem together in the right order so that it makes sense

For the next stage, select five or six words which appear in the song and display them to the class; these, too, can be identified by colour. Ask the children to listen carefully to the song again, and then tell you in which order the five or six chosen words are sung. A variation on this is to select five words from the song, plus two which are **not** in the song, then ask the children to listen carefully once more and to find the two words which do not appear in the song text.

This activity is always very much enjoyed by children, and they often ask if they can repeat a particular activity, in a similar way to asking for a favourite story to be read again. They will ask for particular songs by name and will want to complete the jigsaw puzzles sometimes in groups and sometimes on their own. It is well worthwhile making sets of favourite songtexts to store in a bank of resources which can be used regularly. For each song, photocopy the text on to many different coloured sheets of paper. This avoids problems if pieces of the puzzle from one group get muddled up with pieces from another group, as it is easy to see to which set the pieces belong. When the text has been photocopied on to different coloured sheets, laminate each sheet before you cut it up inot sections, as in this way it can be used again and again.

You can then make differentiated sets of puzzles from the same song text. The easiest puzzles will be those in which each verse is on one piece of puzzle. More difficult puzzles will possibly cut out two lines at a time, and the most difficult will be those which have the smallest pieces. The children will want to perform these puzzles regularly, and they will be able to decide for themselves whether they want to keep trying the 'easiest' version, or whether they would like to tackle the more difficult ones. Each time they try this activity, the learners will notice more features about the language, both aurally and visually. Use the listening post to allow individual or small groups of children to listen to songs and do the jigsaw puzzles independently of the class. This activity provides children with opportunies to practise re-telling stories (through song) in sequence.

Listening to such songs regularly allows learners to hear rhyming patterns and to identify rhyming words in the text. Some will be able to use these words to create their own rhyming patterns, and others will even be able to create their own poems using some of the rhymes and conventions from the songs and poems which they hear regularly.

USING TEXTS TO REINFORCE GRAMMATICAL AWARENESS

When working at sentence level, children will be developing an awareness of grammatical concepts. Using texts can provide a context for further practice. Choose a paragraph from a story with which the children are familiar, and play the *Grammar recognition game* which was described in Chapter 2. When the children have rehearsed the actions sufficiently, change the game slightly. Choose a word type, such as a noun, an adjective, or a verb, and ask the children to make a physical response whenever they hear any word of that type in the story while listening to it.

For example, ask the children to place their hands on their head every time they think they hear a noun (including proper nouns) in the following piece of text:

> «Ah! Ces sales couches!» disait la princesse.
> «Une seule solution: il faut aller sur ton p'tipot», répondait la reine.

Similarly, ask the children to 'walk on the spot' whenever they hear a verb in this piece of text:

> Quelque part au plus profond des mers vivait un poisson. Mais ce n'était pas un poisson ordinaire: c'était le plus beau poisson de tous les océans.

When the children are used to responding to one part of speech within a text, ask them to respond to more than one. For instance, they could place their hands on their head when they hear a noun, and wave one hand in the air when they hear an adjective, in the following piece:

> Bientôt il ne resta plus à Arc-en-ciel qu'une seule écaille brillante.
> Il avait distribué toutes les autres! Et il était heureux, vraiment heureux!

USING NON-FICTION TEXTS

A wide range of non-fiction texts is accessible to learners through a foreign language, such as graphs, letters, diagrams, recipes, strip cartoons, advertisements, instructions and weather forecasts. Activities which allow children to identify various types of text, in a foreign language, can be performed regularly and at different stages of development. Give the children, in pairs or small groups, old newspapers and magazines in the foreign language and set them a challenge, to be completed over the course of a week, for example:

Can you find …

- a recipe;
- a weather forecast;
- instructions for making or doing something;
- a letter;
- an advertisement.

Examples of such text types can be displayed in the classroom, or be kept in the children's foreign language folders or exercise books. As they will have identified a variety of types of non-fiction text, probably not by understanding the body of the text itself, a useful discussion can ensue in which the children can explain which features of the text they noticed which led them to understand what type of text it was. For example, a recipe can often be identified by some of the following features:

- a picture of the finished dish;
- a sequence of pictures showing the dish at different stages if preparation;
- a list of ingredients;
- a list of instructions which explain the procedure for making the dish, often numbered;
- a preparation time or cooking time;
- a number indicating the temperature of the oven.

Similar challenges can be offered to the children if they have access to the Internet. There are many suitable sites for children to explore (see the NACELL website on www.nacell.org.uk). For example, can you find:

- a school timetable;
- a travel timetable;
- a recipe;
- a school handbook (or similar).

If children can learn initially to identify such material, they will already be aware of some of the features of such texts. Their skills can then be further developed by looking closely at different kinds of texts. Try to involve the children actively in each text. A recipe, or a set of instructions, can be acted out using mime to respond to the verbal instructions.

The following recipe for *la crème à l'orange* can be found in *Entraîne-toi* published by Hachette:

 # la crème à l'orange

Préparation : 15 minutes
Pas de cuisson

Pour 4 personnes :
– 2 oranges,
– 6 petits suisses,
– 1 pot de confiture
 d'oranges (ou d'abricots),
– 1 pot de confiture
 de fraises (ou de groseilles),
– 4 cerises confites,

presse-citron, saladier.

1. Coupez les oranges en deux.
2. Pressez les quatre moitiés d'oranges
 avec le presse-citron.
3. Gardez les demi-écorces : elles serviront de coupelles.
 Vous pouvez boire le jus !
4. Dans le saladier, mélangez les petits suisses
 avec 4 cuillerées à café de confiture d'oranges.
5. Remplissez les coupelles avec cette crème.
6. Pour décorer, mettez un peu de confiture
 de fraises et une cerise confite.

Servez bien frais.

Maloux-Braghini S, *Entraîne-toi, CP lecture* (Hachette, 1997)

Together with the children, plan a mime which can illustrate the meaning of each instruction, and practise these. Play physical response games in which you call out any of the instructions in the recipe (in random order), and the class must respond by miming. Give the children opportunities to read the recipe aloud with you so that they become familiar with the sound of the phrases and also with the text.

Play a timed game: with the children sitting in a circle, place seven flashcards randomly in the middle of the circle, each containing one of the written instructions from the recipe. Challenge small groups of children to come into the cicle and place the cards in the correct order in the fastest time.

Finally, allow the children to make the *crème à l'orange*, by following the recipe from the French text. This is an occasion when you could enlist the help of the foreign language assistant, sixth-formers from a local secondary school, and any other French-speaking adults, who could each work with a small group of children to produce a culinary masterpiece! Take photographs at each stage of the preparation, and incorporate these into a wall display, which shows the text of the recipe alongside pictures illustrating each stage of execution.

Let the children use their word-processing skills to type out the recipe, and possibly to import scanned or digital photographs into their work. A copy of this can be put into each child's French folder, and also sent to a partner class abroad.

Children may also be able to locate information about a topic in an encyclopaedia or other reference book, a CD-ROM or the Internet. The following diagram and explanation of the life-cyle of the ladybird comes from *Entraîne-toi* by Hachette:

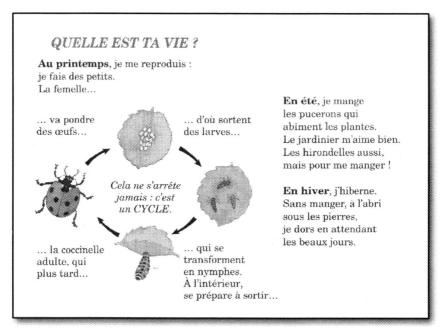

Maloux-Braghini S, *Entraîne-toi, CP lecture* (Hachette, 1997)

The text for each stage of the life cycle can be initially read aloud and later learned by heart, and performed by the class in the style of a *Mexican wave* (see Chapter 2, p36). For this *Mexican wave* divide the whole class into four sections and give each group of children one part of the lifecycle to recite. When the 'script' is more confidently known, divide the class into five groups and repeat the process. This time, the children will find themselves reciting a different part of the lifecycle when they next have a turn. As a written record, allow each child to copywrite the text to match the diagram for each stage of the life cycle. This writing can be achieved using ICT if desired.

USING THE INTERNET TO DEVELOP READING AND WRITING SKILLS

A wealth of authentic, up-to-date material is available nowadays through the Internet. The choice of websites is enormous – from tourist information to football teams; from school home pages to those produced by individual children. Such material has direct appeal to pupils, especially in those cases where it has been written by children for children. Pupils are encouraged to read either for pleasure or for information and there are sometimes opportunities to send back a message to the original author.

It will generally be more practical to download material in order to make hard copies or overhead transparencies, rather than use the material 'live'. You may find it necessary to adapt the material, depending on the language level of your pupils and the aims of your planned activity.

If you are lucky enough to have a linked school abroad, do check whether they have access to Internet, as this can be an exciting way of keeping in touch. Year 6 pupils in a south west London primary school recorded impressions of a visit to their French partner school, including art work, photographs and written accounts in both languages on their website. This was accessed by the French pupils who responded similarly after their visit to London.

We suggest in this chapter a short but by no means exhaustive list of websites that we have found useful, just to get you started. These in turn will lead you on to other links. In order to save time, it is a good idea to bookmark a small selection of favourites, so that you can revisit them on a regular basis and see what updates have been made. When selecting material for use with your pupils, you might find it useful to bear the following six key questions in mind:

- How appropriate is the subject content?

- How appropriate is the language content?

- What adaptation of the material will be required?

- What prior knowledge will the pupils need?

- What knowledge will the pupils gain?

- What follow-up activities will be possible?

Taking some examples of material from the Internet, we can consider these key questions in more detail:

HOW APPROPRIATE IS THE SUBJECT CONTENT?

Food is always a topic of interest to pupils and even a simple recipe in the target language has direct appeal. The recipe for *Fraises au sucre* illustrated here is an example of the kind of text that many children find motivating and are drawn to read. As you can see, it contains the date and also the names of the authors. As pupils know that the extract is not from a text book or something made up by the teacher, it does have an immediacy about it. In this case, the authors' names are underlined, which means that on clicking there, an automatically 'addressed' message slip appears for the reader to send a reply. This type of recipe can easily be prepared in the classroom, with pupils working from the written instructions, as it requires no actual cooking. Linguistically, it offers consolidation of nouns and introduces some commands. Pupils have the chance of reading the very commonly used phrase '*Bon appétit*' in context. The piece of advice '*C'est meilleur avec ...*' can be adapted for other situations. An alternative to pupils preparing the recipe can be for them to illustrate it – this demonstrates their comprehension just as well. Subsequent written work can involve sending back a reply. You might wish to give the children certain key phrases to use, such as: '*J'ai goûté*' or '*J'ai aimé*'. Pupils may wish to send back a recipe of their own, which will give them the opportunity to use some of the language gleaned from the original source material.

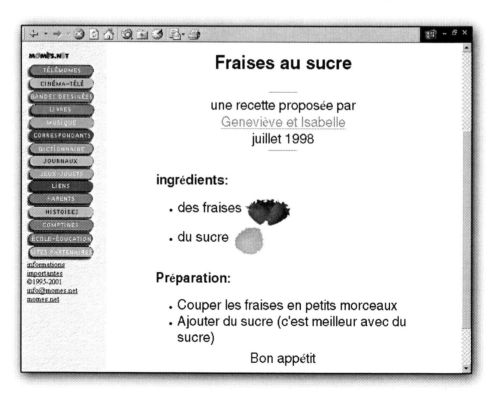

CILT

HOW APPROPRIATE IS THE LANGUAGE CONTENT?

If you decide to supplement your existing materials on a particular topic with pages taken from the Internet, you might find that you need to spend some time looking at different sources before making your choice.

It is important that the language used in the material is of a level appropriate to your pupils. Consider the page from the Marie Curie primary school, for example. It contains some useful photographs of the school buildings which could provide stimulus for comparison with British schools. The text, however, offers facts and figures more likely to interest an adult reader. The language contains educational jargon and abbreviations that would not necessarily appeal to youngsters. Rather than spend time adapting this material, you might prefer to look elsewhere on this occasion.

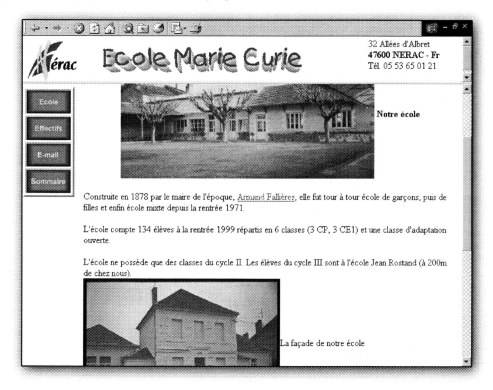

An example from a more child-friendly school website is shown on the following page. It is produced in a large, attractive print and although probably written by an adult, the sentences are short and avoid jargon. Photographs of the school buildings also include shots of the children. The text is written in a variety of colours, so if you can print in colour, it would make an attractive overhead transparency for some shared text work. The extract shown here could link in with geography and map work– finding out where the school is and what the '25' signifies.

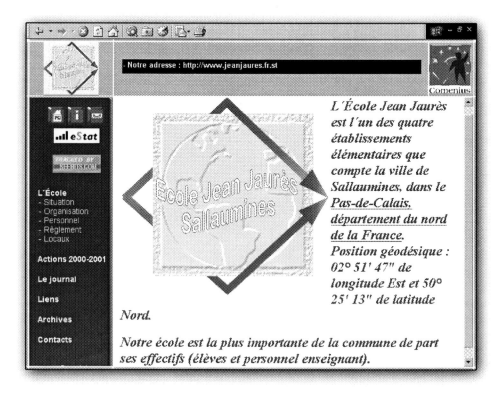

Notre adresse : http://www.jeanjaures.fr.st

L'École Jean Jaurès est l'un des quatre établissements élémentaires que compte la ville de Sallaumines, dans le Pas-de-Calais, département du nord de la France. Position géodésique : 02° 51' 47" de longitude Est et 50° 25' 13" de latitude Nord.

Notre école est la plus importante de la commune de part ses effectifs (élèves et personnel enseignant).

It is of course possible, in both of the above examples, to send back an e-mail reply to the authors!

WHAT ADAPTATION OF THE MATERIAL WILL BE REQUIRED?

There are times when you will find that something that you would really like to use needs to be adapted to suit the particular audience or purpose. As a general rule, anything that is going to involve you in a lot of extra work is not worth it. You will probably be able to find something more suitable elsewhere. An exception to this might be if the source was your partner school abroad, for example. Sometimes, however, you might find a piece of text that is really suitable for your needs but the presentation is off-putting. The page from Bryan M. is an example. The text is a useful one – he writes about himself, his family and hobbies. Simply retyping the text in a bigger font and correcting the minor spelling error would make it much more accessible. Again, you could present this to the class using the overhead projector for shared reading and a stimulus to oral work. This could then lead on to your pupils making up their own texts using this as a model. The page taken from Thomas' website illustrates another example that would require no adaptation. The presentation is clear, there are photographs and the text is both short and relevant.

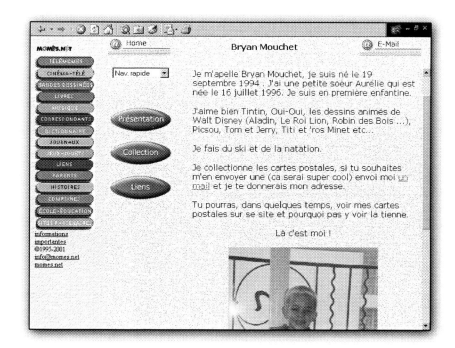

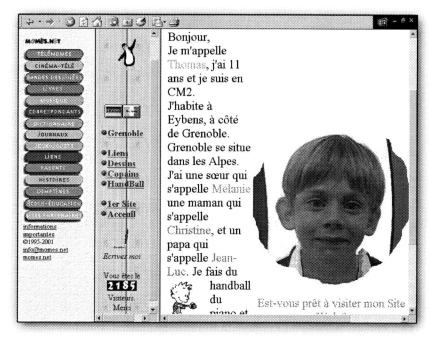

WHAT PRIOR KNOWLEDGE WILL THE PUPILS NEED?

The *'Trempettes de Shreddies'* recipe is a fun example of a text containing a mixture of familiar and unknown language. The recipe itself is so disgusting that children are generally compelled to figure it out!

When approaching this text, learners with some experience of recipes written either in English or the foreign language will find the layout familiar. They will know that recipes usually have the ingredients listed at the top and be aware that these will be followed by the instructions. In this example, some dictionary work is likely to be needed for *beurre d'arachides,* but the notion of 'Shreddies' should need no explanation! The key words here are *assiette* and *trempes.* They would need to have been pre-taught or could be mimed to the group. The explanation of what 'Shreddies' look like gives the opportunity for discussion on cultural differences and why this would need to be explained to a certain audience. In order to make the most of the decription, the adjectives *gauffrées*, *carrée* and *plates* would need to have been covered previously.

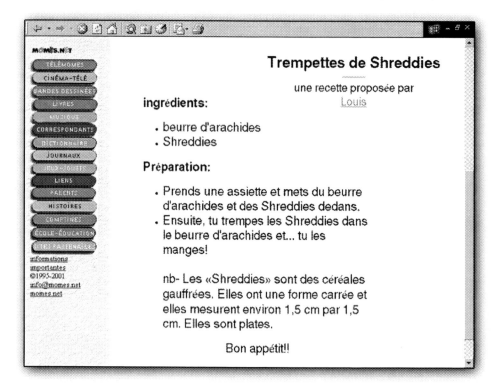

WHAT KNOWLEDGE WILL THE PUPILS GAIN?

The Internet can be a convenient way of accessing rhymes and poems, some written by children and therefore not otherwise easily obtainable. It would be up to you to decide when and if to introduce the written text to your pupils. Many ideas for using poetry have of course been explored elsewhere in this book and could be applied to *Le coquillage.* The outcomes for pupils from working on this poem would be twofold. Firstly, their knowledge of adjectives would be enriched – some would be learned for the first time but other familiar ones (such as *beau* and *gros*) would be consolidated. Secondly, pupils' awareness of the rhythms and sounds of French would be developed by this poem. It is a good poem to learn off by heart and recite aloud, as it combines the element of repetitiveness with single rhyming words. In this example, a message can be sent back to the author, thus providing the opportunity to send an illustration or to add more lines, in French or English.

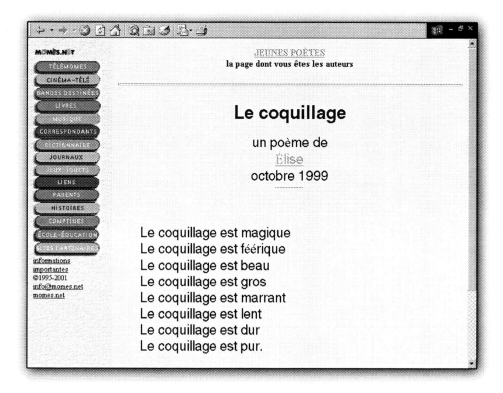

WHAT FOLLOW-UP ACTIVITIES WILL BE POSSIBLE?

As we have seen, there are many activities resulting from stimulus material taken from the Internet that will extend pupils' literacy development:

- sending a reply to the author;
- creating a web page;
- reading for information;
- reading for pleasure;
- making or doing something;
- writing a continuation of the story or poem;
- creating a completely new text.

So how to get started? We list below some websites that we have found useful. This is to give you just a flavour and is by no means exhaustive! You will no doubt soon be able to add your own favourites:

Search engines

French	www.yahoo.fr
German	www.yahoo.de
Spanish	www.yahoo.es

Football teams

Marseille	www.olympiquedemarseille.com
Bayern Munich	www.fcbayern-net.de/index1.html
Real Madrid	www.yrl.co.uk/~gonzalo/rm/9697

Embassies/Cultural services

Francealacarte	www.francealacarte.org.uk
Centro Virtual Cervantes	http://cvc.cervantes.es
Spanish Education Office, Washington	www.spainembedu.org

Websites for children

French magazine for children aged 8–11	www.apreslecole.fr/index.html
Activities in French based on clothes and animal puzzles	www.roptor.com/yeh/
Various activities in French	www.cybermomes.net
Activities and information on citizenship and democracy in France	www.junior.senat.fr
School related material in German	www.schulweb.de
German language search engine for children	www.blinde-kuh.de

CILT

Conclusion

The ideas contained in this Young Pathfinder aim to show teachers a range of methodology which will help to develop children's literacy, no matter which language they are working in. The authors hope that from these beginnings teachers will develop new ideas, which they can take forward and incorporate into their own planning.

It is an important realisation for children that literacy is not confined inside only one language, but exists in all languages. Many young children are bilingual and will already enjoy enormous benefits by making links between their own language and English. It is important that monolingual children begin to enjoy some of the same benefits.

It is hoped that if children's interest in language and literacy is awoken at an early age, they will have the motivation to continue to make language and literacy links throughout the rest of their lives.

Appendix 1: Useful sources

BOOKS CONTAINING POEMS, RHYMES & SONGS

Petites chansons pour tous les jours (Nathan). Contains 66 traditional songs. An accompanying cassette contains a selection of 30 of the songs.

Poésies, comptines et chansons pour Noël (Gallimard Jeunesse). Poems, songs and rhymes on a Christmas theme. Available with audio CD or cassette.

Phonétines (Flammarion-Père Castor). Collection of poems, each of which focus on a particular phoneme. Available with audio cassette.

Être une poule mouillée (Actes Sud Junior). Poems based on French expressions.

101 poésies et comptines (Bayard). Poems based around letters of the alphabet, vowels, consonants and phonemes.

Petit chat perdu (Flammarion-Père Castor). French reading book.

Ein Wiesel saß auf einem Kiesel (Langenscheidt). A selection of German poems.

VIDEOS

'Au Clair de la Lune', Série-télé *'Mon âne'*, Volumes 1 & 2. Available from: Folimage, 6 allée Jean Bertin, 26000 Valence. France. Fax: 75 43 06 92
    Traditional songs with the handwritten text displayed at the bottom of the screen.

Chansons Henri Dès en images. Available from Folimage (as above)
    Thirteen songs sung by Henri Dès, animated with plasticene models. Song text is shown on the screen.

Mr. Ficelle Fun French. Available from Pop English Creations, 22 rue Léoplod Bellan, 75002 Paris. Tel: +33 1 40 26 52 45. Fax: +33 1 40 26 63 35
    Animated songs about colours, numbers, prepositions, shapes & the alphabet.

CD-ROMS

The Cat Came Back (Sanctuary Woods). Suggested age range: Years 1–4. Ref: USGCATPE091095. Languages: English, French

Word Stuff. Suggested age range: KS 1. Ref: Sanctuary Woods POINW05030995. Languages: English, French, German

Bambolo. Suggested age range: Nursery, Reception. Available from: Julia Emily Software, Chambéry, France. E-mail: 106606.3053@compuserve.com. Languages: English, French, Italian

Hexaglot Glotto 5. Suggested age range: Years 2–4. Available from: Hexaglot GmbH, Vertriebsleitung Software, Sportallee 41, 22335 Hamburg, Germany. Languages: English, French, German, Italian, Spanish

All-in-one language fun (Syracuse). Suggested age range: KS 2. Languages: English, French, German, Spanish, Japanese

Mon premier dictionnaire supergénial, My first incredible amazing dictionary, Mein erstes Lexikon (Nathan/Dorling Kindersley/Duden). Suggested age range: KS 2. Languages: English, French, German, on separate CDs

Les surprises de Boub, Le goûter de Margot, Le corbeau et la sorcière, Le jour de Charlotte, Le mystère des lézards (Hatier). Suggested age range: KS 2. Ref: 9 782218 71658 4. Language: French. Five separate CD-ROMS, each with an accompanying reading book, with differentiated activities for children learning to read French.

READING BOOKS

Vahle F and H Heine, *Die Farben* (Middelhauve). Ref: 3-7876-9188-X

Pfister M, *Der Regenbogenfisch.* Ref: 3-314-00733-7

Pfister M, *Arc-en-ciel.* Ref: 3-314-20951-7

Ross T, *Je veux mon p'tipot (I want my potty).* Ref: 2-07-050643-6

AUDIO CDS (SONGS SUNG BY NATIVE SPEAKERS)

Any songs by:
Henri Dès – see website www.henrides.com
Detlev Jöcker – see website www.menschenkinderverlag.de
Rosa Léon

French and German audio CDs and cassettes can by purchased over the web through: www.amazon.fr, www.fnac.com and www.amazon.de

In French, the alphabet is available on the videos *Pilote* and *Mr Ficelle,* in German on the video *3,2,1 – Los!* and in Spanish on the video *Tu y yo.* Audio-cassettes containing the alphabet in French are LJR's *Chante en français,* and in German the tape which accompanies *Tamburin 1.*

STORYTELLING PACKS

Hallam C, *Petites histoires 1* (LJR Educational, 1993)

Hallam C, *Petites histoires 2* (LJR Educational, 1994)

Joyeux Noël (LJR Educational, 1995)

Mireylees J, *Trois petit contes* (2001, Merryman resources)

Tierney D and F Humphreys, *French storytelling resource pack* (Nelson Thornes, 1998)

Appendix 2: Alphabet lists

A

abeille, abominable, agneau, aile, ami, an, âne, ange, anglais, Angleterre, animal, août, araignée, arbre, arriver, assiette, atlas, auberge, automne, autruche, avancer, avion, avril

B

bague, baguette, baignoire, baleine, ballon, barrière, bateau, beau, bébé, bec, belle, berceau, berger, beurre, bicyclette, bijou, biscotte, biscuit, bizarre, blanc, bleu, boire, bois, boîte, bol, bon, botte, bouche, bouton, branché, bravo, briller, brioche, brun, bûche, bûcheron

C

cabri, cacher, cage, calme, caméléon, camion, campagne, canard, canari, caresse, carotte, carré, cassis, castor, catastrophe, cent, centime, , centimètre, cercle, chaise, chambre, champ, chanson, chanter, chapeau, chaperon, chat, château, chatouiller, chaud, cheval, chèvre, chien, chocolat, ciel, cinq, coccinelle, cochon, colle, colorier, commencer, compter, comptine, consonne, corbeau, corps, couleur, couper, courir, couronne, couteau, crapaud, crayon

D

danger, dangereux, date, dauphin, demi, décembre, dessin, dessiner, deviner, dictionnaire, différent, difficile, dimanche, dîner, dix, doigt, donner, dormir, doucement, drapeau, drôle

E

école, écouter, éléphant, encore, encyclopédie, enfant, enrhumé, ensemble, épouvantable, est, estomac, été, étoile de mer, étonnant, étrange, extraordinaire

F

facile, famille, fatigué, faux, femme, fenêtre, ferme, fermé, fête, feuille, feutre, février, fini, fleur, flotter, fourchette, fourmi, fraise, frère, froid, fruit, furet, furieux

G

gâteau, girafe, glace, glaçon, goéland, grand, grenouille

H

habiter, hamster, hélicoptère, heure, heureux, hibou, hier, hippopotame, hiver, horrible, houx, huit

I

identique, impair, important, impossible

J

jacinthe, jambe, janvier, jardin, jaune, jeudi, jouet, jour, joyeux, juillet, juin, jungle

K

kangourou, kilogramme, kilomètre, koala

L

lac, lait, lampe, lapin, lentement, lettre, lézard, libellule, ligne, lion, lire, lit, litre, livre, long, losange, loup, lumière, lune, lundi, lutin

M

madame, magicien, magie, magnifique, mars, mai, maison, majuscule, maman, manger, manteau, marcher, marionnette, mardi, matin, méchant, méduse, menton, mer, merci, mercredi, mère, merveilleux, mètre, meunier, mille, millimètre, million, minuscule, mois, monsieur, monstre, montagne, mot, moulin, mouton, mur, musique

N

nager, neige, neuf, nez, nid, Noël, noir, nombre, non, nord, novembre

O

octobre, œil, oiseau, onze, orange, ordinateur, oreille, orteil, otarie, ouest, oui, ours, oursin, ouvert, ouvrir, ovale

P

page, paf!, paille, pain, pair, panier, papa, papier, papillon, Pâques, pardon, parler, pelle, père, perroquet, petit, panthère, phrase, piano, pièce, pied, pierre, plafond, plage, plouf!, pluie, poche, poème, poète, point, poisson, pomme, pouce, poule, prince, princesse, printemps, puce

Q

quart, quatorze, quatre, question, queue, quinze

R

raisin, ranger, rectangle, reculer, règle, reine, renard, renne, requin, rêve, rien, rivière, robe, roi, rond, rouge

S

sac, sage, saison, salut, sandwich, sapin, sauter, seau, seize, semaine, sept, serpent, siècle, six, sœur, soir, soleil, souris, sorcière, stylo, septembre, samedi, sud

T

table, tableau, tambour, téléphone, terrible, tête, timide, toit, tortue, toucher, treize, triangle, triste, trois, trousse, tiroir

U

uniforme, utile

V

vache, vallée, ver de terre, verbe, vendredi, vert, ville, vingt, virgule, visage, vite, voiture, vrai

W

wagon, week-end, wigwam

X

xylophone

Y

yacht, yack, yaourt, yeux

Z

zèbre, zéro, zoo

CILT

A

acht, Affe, alle, alt, Ameise, April, Arm, Atlas, Auge, August, Auto

B

Bad, Ball, Banane, beginnen, Bein, Birne, Blatt, blau, Blume, Boden, böse, Buch, Bus

C

Café, Clown, Computer

D

Dach, Dachs, Datum, Daumen, Delphin, Deutsch, Dezember, Dienstag, Donnerstag, drei, Dreieck

E

eins, Elefant, elf, Engel, England, englisch, Esel, essen, Eule

F

Familie, Februar, Filzstift, Finger, Fisch, Flugzeug, Foto, Frau, Fräulein, Freitag, froh, Frosch, Fuchs, fünf

G

Gabel, Garten, gelb, Geschwister, gestern, Gramm, groß, gut

H

Hahn, halb, Hand, Haus, Henne, Herbst, Herr, heute, Hexe, hier, Himmel, Hubschrauber, Hut

I

ich, Insekt, Insel

J

ja, Jahr, Jahrhundert, Januar, Joghurt, Juli, Juni

K

Kalb, kalt, Kamel, Kaninchen, Karotte, Katze, Kerze, Kind, Kinn, klatsch!, klein, klopfen, Knie, Knopf, König, Königin, Kopf, Korb, krach!, Kuckuck

L

Lampe, leer, lesen, Licht, Lied, links, Löwe

M

machen, Mai, März, Maus, Meerschweinchen, Milch, Mittag, Mittwoch, Monat, Mond, Montag, Morgen, Möwe, Mund, Mutter, Mutti

N

Nacht, Name, Nase, natürlich, Nebel, nein, neu, neun, nicht, nichts, November, null, Nummer, nützlich

O

oben, Obst, offen, Offizier, öffnen, Ohr, Oktober, Orange, Osterei, Ostern, Österreich

P

Paar, paff!, Panther, Papagei, Papier, Park, Pelikan, Pfeffer, Pferd, Pflanze, Pfund, phantastisch, Piano, Pinguin, plumps!, Prinz, Prinzessin, Puppe

Q

Quadrat, Quatsch!

R

Ratte, Rattenfänger, Raupe, rechnen, Rechteck, rechts, Regen, Regenbogen, richtig, Ruhe, rund

S

Sack, Salz, Samstag, Sand, Satz, Schaf, Schere, Schiff, Schloss, Schmetterling, Schnecke, Schnee, Schneemann, schneiden, schneien, schnell, Schokolade, schön, Schornstein, schreiben, Schuh, Schule, Schulter, schwarz, Schwein, schwimmen, sechs, sechzehn, See, sehen, September, sieben, singen, Sonne, Sonntag, spielen, Spielzeug, Spinne, springen, Storch, Stück

T

Tafel, Tag, tanzen, Tasse, Taube, Teddybär, Tee, Teich, Telefon, Teppich, Tisch, toll, Tomate, Tür

U

Uhr, und, unten

V

Vater, Vati, Verb, vier, Viereck, viereckig, Viertel, vierzig, Vogel, Vokal, voll

W

Wald, Wand, warm, Wasser, Weihnachten, Wind, windig, Winter, Woche, Wolf

X

Xylophon

Y

Ypsilon

Z

Zählen, Zähne, Zauberer, Zebra, Zeh, zehn, zeichnen, Zucker, zusammen, zwei, Zwerg, zwölf

A

abajo adiós, alfombra, amarillo, años, aquí, ayer, azul

B

balón, bici, bien, blanco, bocadillo, bolí

C

caballo, cartera, casa, cierto, cinta, colorear, cumpleaños

D

deporte, día, dibujar, decir

E

eligir, enfermo, escribir, escuchar, escuela, español, estupendo

F

fácil, falda, fantástico, fecha, fenomenal, flecha, fútbol

G

galleta , ganador, gato, grapadora, gris

H

hablar, hacer, hermano, hola, hora

I

imaginar, inglés, intercambio

J

jardín, juego

K

kilo

L

lado, lápiz, leer, libro, lista, lunes

M

madre, malo, mañana, marrón, mascota, mejor, mesa, miércoles, montar, mucho, música, muy

N

naranja, negro, niña, niño, nombre, número

O

ordenador, oreja, otro

P

página, pájaro, patinar, patio, pero, perro, pez, piso, puerta

Q

quién, queso

R

rápido, regla, reloj, repuesta, rojo, rotulador

S

sacapuntas, salir, semana, si, silla, señalar, sobre.

T

tarde, tarta, tele, tengo, terrible, tortuga, tu

U

último, uno

V

verde, vez, viernes

X

xilofón

Y

y, yo, yogur

Z

zapato, zumo

cilt